THE
MASSILLON TIGERS:
15 for 15

THE
MASSILLON
TIGERS:
15 for 15

BY

DAVID LEE MORGAN, JR

FAYETTEVILLE MAFIA PRESS

The Massillon Tigers: 15 for 15
© 2020 David Lee Morgan, Jr.

Book designed by Scott Ryan
Cover & Chapter heading designed by Wayne Barnes
Back Cover Design/Photo by Scott Ryan
Professional photos by Rocky Dorsey
Section Sketches by Dan Studer

Story Editor: Scott Ryan
Copy Editor: David Bushman
Assistant Copy Editor: Alex Ryan

Published in the USA by Fayetteville Mafia Press
Columbus, Ohio

Contact Information
Email: fayettevillemafiapress@gmail.com
Website: fayettevillemafiapress.com

ISBN: 9781949024166
eBook ISBN: 9781949024173

*This book is dedicated to my wife, Jill; my parents,
"Sonny" and Gwen Morgan; my family and friends;
and to all of you who know the importance of
looking for the good inside of everyone.*

CONTENTS

REGULAR SEASON (Second Half)

POSTSEASON

Foreword
by
Jim Tressel

Former Ohio State University head football coach and current president of Youngstown State University

David Morgan was a student journalist during my tenure as head football coach at Youngstown State University. David was an ambitious and outgoing young man, and because he covered the football program for the school newspaper, we began to build a relationship that has turned into a thirty-plus-year friendship. David has been a difference maker to thousands of people through his skill as a writer and his enthusiastic interaction as a teacher and coach.

When David asked if I would write the foreword for this book, I didn't hesitate, not only because of my friendship with David, but also because of my close ties to, and fond memories of, the Massillon Tigers.

Throughout my life I have taken tremendous pride in the fact that I too was and am a Massillon Tiger. When I was a youngster, my dad, Lee Tressel, was the head football coach of the Massillon Tigers, and my memories of living on Seventeenth Street NE are fond. My first introduction to a true rivalry came at a very young age, as I had a front-row seat to the Massillon-versus-McKinley battles. It certainly served me well, as I would many years later find myself immersed in the Ohio State-versus-Michigan excitement. Fortunately, we had some Massillon Tigers, like Devin Jordan and Justin Zwick, so we had the advantage.

The Tressel family is especially proud of some of the great traditions that our dad started at Massillon High School, such as the Sideliners Club and the presentation of the "rose" at the year-end banquet. My dad was always looking for ways to make the Massillon Tiger experience special for the players, coaches, families, and entire Massillon community.

The opportunity for David to coach at Massillon Washington High School is one that I am so glad he has experienced. The impact of the teacher/coach is extraordinary. Billy Graham once said that "a high school coach impacts more kids in a year than a pastor does in a lifetime." David Morgan has now had that thrill and impact.

One time I heard a boxer say that "adversity is the best sparring partner." Many of my best teams at Youngstown State and Ohio State became champions due to the fact that they endured and learned from adversity and disappointment. It will be fun to watch as the players, coaches, and entire Massillon community enter this new decade and build on the accomplishments and lessons from the terrific Tigers of 2019.

It is a belief of mine that our great nation is, in part, so great due to high school football being such a mainstay in our culture. The friendships and brotherhood built, the work ethic and discipline refined, and the TEAM at the center of all activity are truly an advantage that few other nations enjoy. Nothing galvanizes the cities and towns of America like the marching band, the fans, and the passionate players and coaches on game day.

I am very proud of what David has accomplished in his professional career as an author, journalist, and especially as a high school teacher.

Introduction

In my past life as a sportswriter, I wrote for many newspapers, with my tenure at the *Akron Beacon Journal* being the longest. I've covered LeBron and wrote the first biography about him, titled *LeBron James: The Rise of a Star*. I've covered the Indians in the World Series; spring training in Winter Haven, Florida; the Major League All-Star Game in Cleveland. I was the beat writer for the Cleveland Cavaliers, covered Michael Jordan at the United Center, the Browns' first game back in '99 at Cleveland Browns Stadium, the Women's NCAA Basketball Final Four and national championship game with Rutgers winning it all against the Tennessee Lady Volunteers, and so many other amazing sporting events. I say all of that to explain that being a member of the Massillon Washington High School football coaching staff—as the varsity running backs coach during the 2019 season—was one of the greatest sports experiences I've ever had, because it went well beyond sports. As a former journalist who decided to become a teacher and coach, I was blessed to be hired by the Massillon City School District to teach English, writing workshop, and journalism at Washington High School, located in Northeast Ohio. That blessing continued when Head Coach Nate Moore gave me the opportunity to join his staff.

The entire experience was incredible, and what I loved most was that I truly became part of a family. We loved and supported each other, even when things didn't go our way. It was all about creating relationships that will last well beyond the confines of Paul Brown Tiger Stadium—or any stadium we played in. These brothers and sisters whom I met during that year will never know how much they meant to me, and how much they contributed to making this a once-in-a-lifetime experience. Throughout the season, there were so many stories of triumph and, in some unfortunate cases, tragedy. Yet this family and community continued to show why they were and always will be so special. I wanted to include every player, every play, and every moment, but that book would be seven hundred pages. Football is a true team sport. It took all of us to accomplish what we did in 2019. If I missed you in the book, it wasn't intentional. We are all Tigers. Thank you, Coach Moore, for the incredible opportunity. I love all you guys.

Photo by Rocky Dorsey

The Massillon student section chants, "I believe that we will win!"

PRESEASON

Sketch by Dan Studer

Chapter 1
The Birth of 15 for 15

At the end of every game our players *and* cheerleaders gathered at midfield at Paul Brown Tiger Stadium to form a circle and do fifteen push-ups, together as one. In the center stood Defensive Line Coach J. P. Simon. He blew the whistle and yelled off the count. "*One. Two. Three.*" With each whistle, the Massillon football team plunged toward the Astroturf and completed another push-up. "*Four. Five. Six.*" The Tiger faithful and supporters—ranging from five thousand to ten thousand fans, depending on the game—bellowed out the count as well. "*Seven. Eight. Nine.*" Four quarters of football had been played. Forty-eight minutes of a physical chess battle had been waged, but there still was work to be done. "*Ten. Eleven.*" This happened at the end of every game. "*Twelve.*" All through preseason. "*Thirteen.*" These fifteen push-ups represented the fifteen games it would take to reach the state championship. Ten regular-season and five postseason games. It was a symbol of togetherness that helped build an even tighter bond for our team and the entire Massillon community. "*Fourteen.*" Tired after the battle, the town, the team, the cheerleaders, the band, and the coaches chanted out in unison: "*Fifteen.*"

But why fifteen?

Coach Simon explained how it all started:

"The 15 for 15 originally started with myself and a former coach, Terrance Roddy, in the weight room a few years ago. We would end every workout with fifteen push-ups. Each rep of the push-up was representative of what it would take to win a state championship—winning fifteen games. The push-ups were supposed to represent how each week would get harder as every push-up got harder, but you had to earn the right to get to week fifteen.

"I blew the whistle with each push-up they did and continuously yelled. The coaches reminded them what it all meant, the fact that everybody gets ten weeks. Even if you don't win one game during those ten weeks of the regular season, *everybody* gets ten weeks. And it's an absolute honor if you get to play that eleventh game, which means you made the playoffs. But then you have to earn week twelve, and week thirteen, and week fourteen, and, God willing, week fifteen. We continued that throughout the winter, summer, and fall.

"The 15 for 15 started [in the off-season] in 2018. After completing the final preseason scrimmage of 2018 against Lakewood St. Edward, a perennial Ohio power, one of our players turned to me and said, 'Coach, we finished everything with fifteen push-ups. We're not going to stop now.' Since then, after every workout, every scrimmage, and every game, we do our fifteen push-ups so that we remember the ultimate goal—to win a state championship.

"What really became special was after a few weeks of us doing this, the fans started to catch on, and by week ten it seemed like the entire home stands was staying to the end of the games to count the push-ups with the team. To me, this was big-time. It was a sign that we were all *One Town, One Team, One Goal*. Everybody knew what we were playing for, and everybody knew we had to win fifteen games. I think the crowd really bought into the concept. When we got into our playoff runs each of the last two years, I had people sending me pictures of their kids and even their grandparents doing fifteen push-ups to signify they were all in with us. It really took on a life of its own, and it was really special. Only somewhere like Massillon would this even be possible.

Photos courtesy of Leanne Shepherd Voshel

Students Seth Voshel (left) and Brandon Craig (right) doing 15 for 15
in the bleachers at the same time as the team.

"The bottom line is we did the push-ups to beat our archrival, McKinley, and to win a state championship. To do that, you had to play all fifteen games. That's why it will always be important to our players, our coaches, and the people in this community. Whatever happens, our goal every year is to play fifteen games and win a state championship. We're Massillon, and that goal, every year, will never, ever, EVER change."

When Coach Simon talks, it makes me want to hit the ground and give him fifteen. It's easy to forget how tired players are after a hard-fought game of football. The players never dragged their feet as they made their way to midfield to do these push-ups. They sprinted there, willing and ready. This is the character of the Massillon Tigers high school football team. The players know what was expected. It's a symbol of determination, yes. But it's also a symbol of their arrogance.

What team allows itself to plan the entire year around the unlikely goal of making the state championship game? Yes, every team in the state of Ohio and the country *hopes* to win a state title, but to chant it out at a preseason scrimmage game? Most coaches give the old cliché after each win: "One game at a time." In Massillon, the state game is the bar. In 2019, there were 107 Division II teams competing to play that final week in the state of Ohio. Only two teams would make it. Massillon screamed out for all to hear—it demanded to be in that game.

The Tigers have won twenty-four state championships in its 127-plus years of playing football, but it has won no state titles since 1970. They have never won a state title since the playoff system was implemented in 1972. In 2018, Massillon did play fifteen games. The team entered that state championship game with an undefeated record. It was the first time the team went 14-0 in its history. They finished the season 14-1, with a loss to four-peat state champion Akron Archbishop Hoban. If Massillon wanted to return to the state game in 2019, Hoban would be standing in its way, along with many other factors that can derail a season.

Despite the odds, Massillon's players started the 2019 season with the same mantra. They will play fifteen games. They will reach the state finals again. But this time, they will win. They will get 15 for 15. They won't just play in fifteen games. They will win fifteen games.

This is the story of the 2019 season's quest to win that fifteenth game. Go Tigers!

The first round of push ups for the first game of 2019.

Chapter 2
Football and Marriage

It was an early morning in August 2019. School was about to start, and I was enjoying my last few days of summer vacation as a teacher at Massillon Washington High School. It is well-known that one of the luxuries of being a teacher is having summers off. I was taking my wife, Jill, to work at Akron Children's Hospital, which I routinely did during the summer, since we lived just five to ten minutes from her job. This gave me ample time to discover new projects I would start and never finish. Before I dropped Jill off at work every morning, we'd stop at Starbucks. She had turned me into a coffee snob. Before I met her I was accustomed to the flavorful, freshly brewed coffee of the local gas station Circle K. As my wife and I got back in my car at Starbucks, I sat on my phone, which was in my back pocket. At this precise moment, when I pulled it out of my pocket to rest it on my console, I noticed the screen read "Coach Nate Moore." He was the head football coach at Massillon and a friend whom I respected for far more than his coaching prowess.

I turned to Jill and said, "Hon, this is Coach Moore, I think I butt-dialed him and he's calling me back. Let me get this and tell him it was a mistake." Jill nodded, so that she didn't interrupt her exquisite first sip of Starbucks coffee. I answered my phone. We didn't drive off; we stayed right there in the parking lot, because I wanted to be, at the least, courteous and answer Coach Moore's call right away. Even though I *assumed* his call was by accident.

I laughed, to defuse that awkward moment we've all experienced when someone calls you back thinking you had something important to tell them.

"Umm, sorry, Coach Moore, I think I butt-dialed you." I said.

"No, you didn't. I called *you*," he said.

"Oh!!" I said, surprised. I mean, why would Coach Moore call me at 7:30 in the morning just as he is preparing for the first scrimmage of the 2019 season—which was that very day?

"What would you think about being our running backs coach this year?" he asked.

This was a question I never thought I would hear in my entire life. Especially given that I hadn't played football since my freshman year in high school and that I came from Warren G. Harding High School, which had a history of loathing Massillon because of past encounters on the gridiron and basketball court. I said nothing. I just couldn't form words.

"Hello?! David, are you still there?!" I was looking at Jill, who heard the question because we were on speaker, and I had no idea how to answer. I finally answered back.

"Umm, what?!! Are you serious? Coach Moore, I don't know anything about coaching running backs at the high school level. I'm not sure how much I can give you or how much I can contribute."

The whole time I was just looking at Jill and shrugging my shoulders like, "What the hell do I do?" She smiled at me with a smile that only a husband would know meant she was not happy about this.

"Yes, I'm serious," Coach Moore said.

Coach Moore explained that last year's running backs coach, Eric Copeland, a quality young man who had played for the Tigers, was moving on. Eric had played the sport hard, because he was from Massillon, learned the game hard, because he was from Massillon. The kids and coaching staff loved him hard, because he was from Massillon.

Coach Copeland had accepted a graduate assistant position at John Carroll University, a Division III school outside of Cleveland, about an hour from Massillon. The offer came in just days before the Tigers' first preseason scrimmage, against Avon, a perennial playoff team that we could face in the playoffs if we made another deep run. We were all happy for Eric and knew it was a great opportunity for him. We wished him the best.

Coach Moore wrapped up the call with "Look, you've coached baseball and basketball at Massillon. The kids know you and really like you. You've had some of them in your class. We could really use you right now."

I was speechless. Jill was also speechless, but her silence was saying a lot.

Let's step back in time for a moment. When I first decided to make the career switch from journalist to high school English, creative writing, and journalism teacher, I knew I wanted to go to a district that needed me. Being an African American male who taught English, I wanted to help all students, but especially black, disadvantaged, and at-risk students. I had earned a bachelor's degree in professional writing and editing with a minor in journalism through the English department at Youngstown State University. Effective writing was always something I enjoyed. I know how important it is for students and their futures. You don't see many black male high school English teachers. I wanted to do what I could to change that. Because of how much I appreciated, loved, and understood the importance of writing, I wanted to share my passion with students in a district where I felt comfortable teaching. Massillon City Schools was it.

When it came to demographics and socioeconomics, Massillon was similar to my hometown of Warren, Ohio. The cities, separated by about sixty miles, were both filled with whites and blacks, Italians and Greeks, you name it. There was Copperweld Steel in Warren and Republic Steel in Massillon. They both had labor unions, third shifts, and orange-red glowing skies at night because of the blast furnaces that for years had helped build the middle class in Northeast Ohio. The disappearances of those industries left the night sky dark and jobs hard to find. At the end of the workweek during the fall, both towns headed to the local high school football stadiums. Admittedly, no town was quite like Massillon with its dedication to the high school football team. The Warren and Massillon football battles started back in 1921. The two teams have faced each other over eighty times, making Warren the second-most-played team in Massillon's history. Second only to the Tiger's greatest rival: the Canton McKinley Bulldogs. So there is no love lost between the two communities.

I can say that becoming part of the Massillon community as an outsider was something special because of how people embraced me once they knew I was sincere about being here. With that said, there were still people who were jealous of me, or indifferent toward me, for whatever reason, but I didn't care. I knew of people who talked about me before they even knew me, and when they heard I was going to be hired they questioned why I was being hired, as if I didn't have the qualifications to become a licensed teacher, which in fact I did have, and had worked my butt off to earn.

Not only that, there were colleagues right in our building, and right on my floor, who would walk right past me, look me dead in the eyes, and yet not say a word to me, making it my job to say hello to them first. I didn't owe them anything. I was just being cordial, friendly, and a team player. The reality was that my job was to be the best teacher I could possibly be, and to make my students and all the students I came in contact with know I loved them and would do anything to help them become successful in and out of the classroom.

When I was hired at Massillon, I was on a mission to do everything I could to help my students at Washington High School with their academic goals, and any other life goals they had. I was going to be there for the students. In fact, during my first four years of teaching at Massillon, I coached junior varsity baseball for two years and freshman basketball for a year. I was the success club adviser, the JV and varsity boys' basketball announcer, the wheelchair-basketball announcer, the organizer of Red Nose Day, the organizer of Akron Children's Hospital "Change Bandit" fundraiser, and the instructor for our school newspaper, the *Tiger Eye News* (tenohio.com.)

But for the 2019-2020 school year, I had decided to take time off from volunteering, and not do a darn thing. Nothing! Jill and I

Photo courtesy of Jill Morgan

Jill, D.J., and me just a few weeks before I got the call that changed my life.

loved being able to head south to Columbus for Ohio State football games in the fall. Then stop at the local mall, Easton Town Center, on our ride back Sunday mornings to shop. Or maybe this year we would go north to Cleveland to watch my Browns or head east to Pittsburgh to watch her Steelers. We wanted to go shopping for gourds, cornstalks, and pumpkins to decorate the front of our house for the fall. All of that fun stuff. That's why I decided to take a year off from everything.

However, there was another reason I was pulling back. We had a new addition to the family. His name was D. J., and what a wonderful baby he was. We both had planned for this bundle of joy a year in advance, and he finally arrived in July. We were instantly in love with him. Was it another child? Oh, no. It was an adorable chocolate Lab puppy that became the center of our lives. I had begged Jill for this puppy, like a little boy, for a full year, and she finally gave in—under one condition: that I would be home to train him. I couldn't wait to take a few years away from coaching and other extracurricular activities and spend more time with Jill and the newest addition to our family. Once you added in our adult children and grandson, Avery, my life was filled with family activities. Everything was planned out perfectly.

Then, Nate called!

I told Coach Moore I was driving Jill to work, but that I would think about it. As soon as I hung up, the next conversation was intense. Jill didn't want me to take the job, and I didn't want to turn down an opportunity to coach at one of the most legendary high school football programs in the country. Even though I had never coached high school football, the fact that I had this chance was something I felt I just couldn't pass up. All I could think about was stepping onto a football field where an average game can bring in around 10,000 fans. But I knew Jill had a lot of family plans for the fall. Plans I had wanted to be a part of . . . up until a few moments ago. It was going to be a tough decision.

After I dropped Jill off, I sat in the parking lot thinking about what transpired. I called Coach Moore back and told him of my interest. He asked if I could meet him and a few other coaches at 1:30 that afternoon in the coaches' office at school. I said, "Of course." However, I was supposed to meet Jill for lunch at noon at the hospital.

I kept both appointments.

While I was having lunch with Jill, she thought the matter was resolved. That could be because I didn't tell her about the meeting I was going to with Coach Moore as soon as lunch was over. My lunch with Jill seemed like a dream, an out-of-body experience. I really didn't hear anything she was saying, because I was afraid of what she was going to say (and do) to me if she found out I was meeting with Coach Moore.

At the meeting with Nate, I was given the opportunity to dig my grave even deeper. Everything he said sounded perfect. I was getting more excited by the moment. I knew that this was a once-in-a-lifetime opportunity. In fact, it would be a one-year opportunity. The only reason I was in this position was because they needed someone right now. I was a living, breathing human who worked at the school and had coached a sport before. Next year they would rightly hire a coach who specialized in running backs. This was one and done. Hmm, I wondered if that would help smooth things over with Jill?

As the meeting wrapped up, Nate informed me that the team pictures were being taken in the next hour. I could pose with the coaches for the photo that would be used in every program for the games that season. Photo day was always a big deal, not only because it was when the players, coaches, cheerleaders, trainers, student managers, and anyone else officially involved with the football program got their pictures taken for the program, but also because it provided the opportunity for our football family to take personal photos that would last a lifetime. "You might as well jump in the picture," Nate said, urging me on. I was already in enough trouble taking this meeting; if I stood in that picture, I would effectively be saying yes. And while I really wanted to take this job, I also really wanted to stay married. I said, "I need to speak with Jill before I make the commitment." I declined to be in the team picture.

When I left my meeting with Coach Moore that afternoon, I told him again that I would talk to Jill when I got home and let him know if I could accept. "Trust me, I totally understand," he said. I picked Jill up from work later that afternoon. When we got home, I told her about the meeting. We discussed the cons. The new puppy that we'd gotten only three weeks before. The same puppy that I said I would take care of. The time with our grandchild. The trips we planned in every direction. The time this commitment would take up. To be a coach at Massillon isn't simply about the two-hour-a-day practice time. It is a twenty-four-hour-a-day job, with texts from coaches, plays to learn, and film to watch. Not to mention that I had zero experience being a running backs coach. I would feel like an impostor. Jill didn't want me to take the job, and rightfully so. I completely understood her point of view. I couldn't be mad at her—it was a valid point.

The pros? Just one. I would be a coach on the Massillon football staff. As a Warren athlete, I had hated Massillon and all it stood for: a proud and successful tradition at the expense of all other local programs, with a large and faithful (perhaps arrogant) fanbase that made any away game feel like home. But in four years of teaching and getting to know the students and the community, I was beginning to understand that it wasn't what it all seemed from the outside. It wasn't about winning. It was about legacy. About history. About family. I could be a part of that family.

I looked at Jill's face. I pet D. J. on the snout. I thought about it, thought about all the cons and the single pro, thought about the sacrifice that Jill made for me in getting a puppy AND the sacrifices she would have to make if I took the job. I called Nate back that night and turned the job down. Nate said he understood. I did the right thing by my family. There was only one thing left to do. To proceed to pout like a baby for the rest of the night. Damn, I wanted it so badly.

Sitting downstairs staring at D. J., I thought of something that hadn't occurred to me all day long. The Massillon-McKinley game! I just passed up a chance to coach in the greatest high school rivalry in the country. The war of 1894. The Massillon Tigers battled the McKinley Bulldogs in week ten, and it was all that mattered in this community. The towns are just twelve miles apart. Beating McKinley was what all football players were measured by in Massillon. I had coached against them in baseball twice. I lost 6-5 and 12-11. I coached against them in basketball and lost in overtime. I had just agreed to pull back from coaching all sports. How could I be a coach at Massillon and *never* beat McKinley? How could I pass up the chance to beat them in football? I was passing up so much. Nate Moore gets his coaches from all around the country. He has traveled to Atlanta to the Nike coaches convention to hire for these positions. Today, he called a former journalist in a Starbucks parking lot. And I was passing. D. J. poked his nose at my feet, but I wasn't anywhere near done pouting yet.

I woke up the next morning and it was the same routine—drive to Starbucks, drop Jill off at work, then go home and find something to do. The car ride was pretty quiet.

Did I mention what a wonderful wife I have? After I dropped Jill off at work, she, unbeknown to me, sent this text message to Becca Moore, Nate's wife:

Jill: Hi Becca! Can you do me a favor? Can you, without David knowing it was me, ask Nate to approach David again about the RB coach if he hasn't already filled the position? I think he declined because of me. 😟

Becca: Yes! Anything for you two!! But just so you know,

Nate is a terrible liar.

Jill: OK! And Nate can tell him I messaged you. Whatever it takes. I want David to do it. I didn't want him to because of our new puppy, etc. But that wasn't fair. I was selfish. He needs to do it. He loves those kids.

Becca: Awww you are so sweet- we need a positive influence like him to be a coach!

And with that, I got another call from Coach Moore asking me to take the job. He informed me that Jill had texted Becca and the light was green. He asked me to meet with him and co-offensive coordinators Jon Mazur and Jarrett Troxler. Now that I knew my wife was behind me 100 percent, my incredible experience of becoming part of the Massillon Tigers' coaching fraternity and my 15 for 15 quest for a state championship began. I wouldn't be in the group photo with the rest of the coaches in the program. I missed that the day I drove home and pouted. But they did put an old black-and-white photo of me next to the coaches that made me look like I was from the Marion Motley era of football. And my name would be listed as a coach. Forevermore, I would be known as Massillon Tigers Running Backs Coach David Lee Morgan, Jr. It never would have happened without Jill. I give thanks to the most supportive wife in the world for putting my dreams first. I am a lucky man.

All I had to do now was learn how to coach running backs at a school that lives and breathes football and is setting its sights on winning a state championship. Oh, boy!

Chapter 3
The Massillon Mystique

You can travel just about anywhere in the country wearing a Massillon T-shirt or hat and a football fan will ask you about the Tigers. If they are from the area, they may yell out a "T-I-G" and your response is always an "E-R-S." This is a cheer heard over and over at every game. The fans on the east side of Paul Brown Tiger Stadium yell "T-I-G." The fans on the west side of the stadium answer with the "E-R-S." This becomes an effective mental advantage that the crowd can use to intimidate an away team going for a third down. The chant can be heard everywhere that fans gather. The town of Massillon has just a little over 35,000 residents and a stadium that holds upward of 18,000. That means there is a seat for every other resident in the city.

As of this writing, Massillon was the all-time-winningest team in Ohio and fifth in the nation. It has been known as the mecca of football ever since legendary coach Paul Brown put Massillon on the football map. Paul Brown is probably one of the greatest men to ever be involved in the game of football, at every level—high school, college, and professional—and he was from right here in Massillon. He was a tactician. He invented the playbook, for goodness sake. Paul Brown was a 1925 graduate of Washington High School and played quarterback for the Tigers. He returned to the school to become the head coach and win six-straight state titles. He went on to Ohio State and coached it to its first national championship. As head coach of the Cleveland Browns (1946-1962), he took players shunned by racist professional-football owners who didn't want any black players. His perspective on the game was that race never mattered, only ability and character. He didn't want anyone on his teams (Massillon, OSU, Cleveland, or the Cincinnati Bengals) who weren't going to accept black players. And for that reason, Paul Brown became legendary when it came to integrating African American athletes into the game of football. He helped to integrate pro football when he signed Hall of Fame running back Marion Motley and Bill Willis to the Browns in 1946. It opened the door for Jackie Robinson. Arguably the greatest running back in National Football League history, Jim Brown, played for Paul Brown in Cleveland.

Paul Brown, while being the most famous Massillon Tiger, is just one chapter in the book on Massillon football. There have been documentaries made about the team, ESPN news reports, and coverage in *Sports Illustrated*. If you know football, you know Massillon. The town where every baby boy born is given a football. In a country that is obsessed with sports, what's not to love about Massillon? Well, maybe ask the rest of Ohio. Outside of the city limits of Massillon, there is a stark difference in the way the Tigers are perceived. There is no doubt that just about every team that ever played Massillon would pay hard money to never have to hear that "T-I-G" chant EVER again. Well, no one around the Massillon program is taking them up on that offer.

Why does this Massillon Mystique seem to mystify so many people who don't understand this phenomenon? And truth be told, it is a phenomenon. Massillonians know it's something ingrained in them. It extends for generations. It's an understanding that the young men on the gridiron are the heart and soul of this city, along with the cheerleaders and the members of the famous Tiger Swing Band. Add the majorettes, and of course Obie, the mascot, whose name is an acronym for "Orange and Black Is Everything." (For many years, a real, live Tiger cub would travel with the band and watch every game from a cage on the sidelines, but animal-rights activists put a stop to that. At the end of every season

Obie the tiger used to watch every game from his cage and then retire to a zoo. It is a tradition that no longer continues.

the cub was donated to a zoo.)

They all represent the city, its values, and the hardworking, blue-collar ethic of the citizens.

Coach Moore said, "You'd be treading in dangerous waters to compare Massillon Tigers football to religion, but if you look at what a church family or a parish does for a community and how that brings people together, I really think it's similar. All these fans have this common goal—black, white, rich or poor, old or young—and every Friday night in the fall they pay homage. It's a community event in a way that's somewhat of a spiritual movement."

He added that the Massillon Mystique wasn't superficial, flashy, or fake:

"Where most teams have just parents and grandparents of the team going to their games, we have generations of families who live and die for Massillon football," Coach Moore said. "We also have people who do not have a direct connection to Massillon. No son or daughter, no niece or nephew, no grandson or granddaughter playing or attending the school anymore. They are just pure Massillon Tiger fans. It's something ingrained in the community, because of how good

21

Massillon was when football was becoming a major sport. Massillon was unbelievable, and it was powerful enough to carry on for decades. And then you fast-forward to the steel mills closing and all the stress put on this community, so what you had was Massillon Tiger football bringing the community together. If you looked around, it wasn't like football was the only thing in town. There were other great things going on in the community, but Massillon Tigers football was in the DNA of people's childhood, and in the DNA of their parents, and in the DNA of their grandparents. So now you have generations of Massillon fans, and that is something so unique. It's simply amazing."

The mayor of Massillon, Kathy Catazaro-Perry, seconded Moore's sentiments about the fans: "I think they hold onto that tradition, and I think that is so important to them. They want the team to win, but it's also about the integrity of the people supporting the team, because the strength of our community is the heart and the excitement for our team. And it's not just our team. We love our Tiger Swing Band as well. Everyone is striving for excellence."

Former Massillon Tiger Andrew David, whose family has long supported the program, knows what being born to be a Tiger is like.

Andrew David sets the record for the longest field goal at PBTS on September 19, 2014.

"Since I could open my eyes, I've been associated with Massillon," he said. "My dad [Jeff] was a coach at Massillon and my grandpa [Paul] had a great relationship and friendship with Paul Brown. So there's a connection with Massillon football and my family before I was even enrolled in the school there."

David was a phenomenal kicker for Massillon from 2011 to 2014. He set a ton of records. He went on to play at multiple esteemed Division I football programs, but it is playing at Massillon that sticks with him most of all. He explained, "There are different rarities you experience playing football, but just being able to run out of the tunnel is one of those feelings that can't compare to anything. I got to run out at 'The Big House' at the University of Michigan. I got to run out of AT&T [formerly Cowboys] Stadium when I was with TCU. And I got to play at 'The Horseshoe' at Ohio State, but I'll tell you firsthand right now: none of those came remotely close to the adrenaline rush of running out of the tunnel onto the field at Paul Brown Tiger Stadium."

Did I forget to mention that Massillon has an indoor football practice field? This is Massillon football. We have the best equipment to match the best coaching staff. Massillon built the Paul L. David Athletic Training Center in 2008, and the building is eighty thousand square feet. It contains a full football field and would rival any college campus's practice area.

David, whose family donated the money for the building said, "The facility alone I think is something that gets people to grow closer. Every time I go in there, I'm still in shock. I've seen some of the best college indoor facilities, and Massillon's rivals some of those spaces that I've

Photos by Rocky Dorsey

The indoor facility where the Tigers practice and sports medicine classes are held.

been in. I think the indoor facility just kind of helps bring everything together, and it's very humbling to know that we have it."

With all that Massillon has, is there a level of arrogance here in Tiger Town? You bet. There has to be, and that will *always* be here. It's a blind, confident arrogance. I say blind because Massillonians don't know they are being arrogant. Critics can say, "How in the world can Massillon be so arrogant when it hasn't won a state championship in football since the playoff system began in 1972?" That question is simple to answer in the minds of those who live here. The community feels an obligation to continue to make this town a successful football town, whether that's right or wrong. The process of striving to win a state championship has never changed. They will always be here, long after we are gone. Our hope is that every year develops a level of excellence that surpasses the previous year's. So, from that standpoint there is a level of unintentional *intentional* arrogance. It's not that every week Massillon looks past its opponent; it's just that every week its opponent is its own past. How do you set a record at a school that has had record-setting players for over a hundred years? Are you competing against the away team or the father who played the same position that you are playing? At the same time, it's a matter of having blinders on and not worrying about what anyone else is saying about us. That's not Massillon. Massillon is about setting a standard that allows us to continue winning—despite not winning a championship since 1970.

Our wide receivers coach, Cale Miller, said, "Anybody who knows anything about football knows what Massillon is all about. Sure, people will say we haven't won a state championship since the playoff system started, but what I've really come to find out is that any place, any program that has had so much success over time like us, people are going to hate it. They're going to hate it because they're not part of it. For us, it's a love affair with the city. It's the greatest love affair with football I've ever come across, and I'm just very blessed to be a part of it."

Defensive Ends Coach Dave Weber, a former Tiger player himself, is an expert on teaching the team what it means to be a Tiger. When asked about Massillon and what it means to wear the orange and black, he said, "Our fan base keeps aging, but those people who are sixty-five, seventy, and seventy-five years old are still walking all the way up into the stands in the double-letter rows because of the group of young men that are out there on that field wearing that uniform. The binding thing in this town is our football team. The economy in many towns in the Midwest like ours have been destroyed with the closing of the steel mills. People left those cities. Here, people may have found jobs outside of Massillon, but they wanted to stay here. We are who we are, and we stay who we are because of the tough people in this town who have persevered for so long. They could have easily given up, moved away, and started a life somewhere else. But they wanted to stay here. So our players owe those people in the stands who stayed here for them. That means our effort always has to be 110 percent, no matter who we're playing, because our community and supporters deserve that."

That is the pressure that is put on the Tiger players, who range in age from fifteen to eighteen. They don't buckle because of it. They were born into it. They have been preparing for this their entire school career. Weber continued, "Our kids come from hugely diverse backgrounds. Some have nobody at home backing them up. We are going to keep fighting until we accomplish the goal of winning a state championship. And then we'll keep fighting to win another. The guys before us have set the bar, and our job each year is to finish what they have done so that the future classes understand how we get here and where we're going."

Even our opponents know what it means and how special it is to compete against Massillon. If you beat the Tigers, you can carry that around with you for a lifetime. Seasoned actor Ray Wise, a Garfield High (Akron, Ohio) alum who is known for his role as Leland Palmer in the television series *Twin Peaks*, lives in Los Angeles and still talks about his days as a member of the Garfield Rams. "We beat Massillon 13-6 in 1963, and right after beating them we were ranked number two in the state because we knocked off the big boys—the Massillon Tigers," said Wise, who was a 180-pound offensive guard back then. "I blocked with my brain instead of my body," he joked. "I could handle those 250-pound big boys from Massillon and Warren because I was quick and I had leverage. I knew what I was doing. I guess that's what is meant by having brains over brawn." Here is an actor who has well over two hundred credits, in projects like *RoboCop*, *Fargo*, and *Fresh off the Boat*, but how he lights up at the chance of talking about beating "the mighty Massillon Tigers" some fifty years later.

Former Massillon captain and defensive lineman Ellery Moore was one of the senior captains featured in the film *Go Tigers!*, a documentary released in 1999 by filmmaker and former Massillon football player Kenneth Carlson. The film showed the heart and soul, and life and breath, of Massillon football through the eyes of the players. "Massillon football really created a purpose for Ellery and gave him reasonable limits," Carlson said. "That was one of the messages of the film, that you can find purpose in different places and that you've got to look for it, and then, once you find it, you've got to work hard to better yourself. That's what Massillon football did for Ellery, and he's a perfect example of that."

I asked Ellery to explain the Massillon Mystique. He paused for a moment to gather his thoughts, then started putting it into words. "If I were to explain the Massillon Mystique in a football sense, most people wouldn't understand how a town of 35,000 people were so crazy and so obsessed over high school football, and it wasn't something like Major League Baseball, the NFL, the NBA, or MLS, where millions and billions of dollars are being generated," he said. "The money doesn't matter. I always talk about Massillon like this: some of the greatest and most unique individuals in the world, Albert Einstein, Michael Jackson, people like that—they were slightly insane, right? They had a level of insanity—a level that was so off-the-wall that nobody understood it. There was something that wasn't right with those individuals. Now, I know people may say, 'What are you talking about, Ellery? That has nothing to do with sports.' I'm talking about the obsession of being great at who and what you are. That's what Massillon is. There's no gray area when it comes to Massillon Tiger football. It's just a full-on, full-bore obsession. We're insane. We're crazy. We cry over Massillon football. We fight over Massillon football. We've even had some that have died for Massillon football."

It may sound dramatic to an outsider, but Ellery is right on target. Ellery has an inspiring way of talking about the Tigers. It's not a surprise that he is one of the local radio broadcasters, along with Ray Jeske, who

In pictures above and below, Tiger fans gather outside the stadium early to tail gate before every home game. The air is filled with open grills and Kraus' Pizza.

call the game every Friday night on ESPN 990 AM in town and on the Internet for Tiger fans who want to follow the games live. Listening to Ellery transported me to a moment I had had after a game late in the season. I was driving home from the stadium. I stopped at a gas station on Wales Avenue, across from the popular Dairy Queen drive-through. I went into the mart to pay for gas and get a bag of chips. There was a grisly looking older white gentleman in front of me in line. He had a scraggly grayish-white beard and was wearing a dusty Massillon cap that looked like he had bought it in 1975. His black jacket matched that age, with shiny material and the faded script "Massillon" written across the chest, separated by the snaps of the orange buttons running from the bottom of the jacket to the collar. The man was polite as could be as he struck up a conversation with me. I assumed he knew I was a coach, because I was wearing my gear.

"Great game tonight, Coach," he said to me.

"Thank you, sir, I appreciate that. Did you go to the game?"

"Oh, you betcha. I usually don't miss any games. It's like a ministry to me," he chuckled. "A ministry of football, like when I used to go out in the yard and throw the ball around with my son. His mom and grandma didn't understand, but deep down inside they did understand, you know what I mean?"

It was as if he was having an out-of-body experience, like he needed a Snickers to pull him back into the real world. He chuckled, reached into his back pocket to pull out his wallet. Before I could politely answer, a black gentleman who was standing behind us asked, "So how *is* the team doing?" He had graduated from Massillon but moved to Columbus and was back in town for the weekend. We all started talking about making a run at a state championship, and the conversation was getting deep. Thankfully we were the only three in the store besides the cashier, and it seemed like nobody was in a rush to leave. The great thing about this conversation was we didn't even know one another, but in that short time we talked like we had been acquainted for years. I don't know their names. I will probably never see them again. It didn't matter what our race was, what our jobs were, what our politics were. We were one. We were Massillon. We were talking about Massillon football. One Team. One Town. One Goal.

Chapter 4
A Crash Course in Coaching

My high school football coaching résumé spoke for itself. There was nothing there. Still, every single coach on staff welcomed me fabulously. I felt good about that initial meeting we had in the football coaches' office in August, less than a month from the start of the season. I sat there with the entire staff knowing I didn't have the same football knowledge they possessed, but I loved that they accepted me into the family. I was confident they would help me through this experience. There was just one condition. Coach Craig McConnell, co-defensive coordinator, said, "You gotta check your ego at the door." He was one of the most intense coaches I have ever come in contact with in my life. He was also the most misread teacher in the school.

People thought Craig was a hard-ass all the time. He wasn't. He was dean of students one year, which meant he had to hand out discipline. So when students (and even some staff) saw him coming down the hall wearing his no-nonsense shirt and tie, and his Chuck Norris facial expression, they got out of his way. He was just doing his job. He later became an assistant principal, and he deserved that position because he was damn good at what he did in his professional capacity off the field.

If McConnell was the peak of confidence, I was the polar opposite. I felt like I had "impostor syndrome," like I was a fraud and didn't belong. I met with Coach Moore and co-offensive coordinators Jon Mazur and Jarrett Troxler, and they gave me the playbook. It was as thick as *War and Peace*. It felt like it had a thousand pages. The coaches were marking up plays on the board and showing me formations and alignments that looked like Einstein's theory of general relativity. I knew at that moment that I may have been in over my head. I looked to the left to see if Bill Belichick was drawing up these plays. I looked to the right to see if Tony Dungy was running our offense. This *was* high school, right? We had already played our first scrimmage, against Avon, so I was already behind the eight ball.

Practice was run with precision right down to the last second. The team gathered in the locker room and everyone got taped up. Special teams headed outside to the field to work on the kicking game while the rest of the team headed to the indoor field.

Once special teams finished up outside, they rejoined the team in the indoor facility. We began our stretches as a team. From there on, Coach Moore had a huge clock on wheels that kept our countdown of thirty-eight, four-minute periods. That's how we ran our practices. It was efficient and scripted, down to the last second. No time was wasted between periods.

I'll be honest, it took me well into the season to understand what we were doing offensively. What was so great about Coach Moore, Coach Mazur, Coach Troxler, and the entire coaching staff was that these guys knew I didn't have much football coaching knowledge, and didn't care, and were always willing to help.

I did reach out to a great source to help me with the first step in coaching. I decided I would call my longtime friend from Youngstown State University Jim Tressel. I had known Coach Tressel since our days at YSU in the mideighties. He became a mentor and eventually a great friend. He was the first person I thought of to ask for coaching advice. I called him and said, "Coach Tressel, I'm coaching the running backs here at Massillon and I have no idea what to do. Can you help me with what I need to teach them?" He congratulated me on my job and summed it up in two words: "Ball control."

My first scrimmage was the following week, on August 16, 2019. We faced off against the Berea-Midpark Titans. My place wouldn't be on the sidelines pacing along with Coach Moore and the players. I would be the "eye in the sky," along with Mike Stone, who coached the fullbacks and tight ends. We were the two offensive coaches in the press box. We sat alongside Craig McConnell and Spencer Leno, who were the co-defensive coordinators in the box. We shared the space with several freshman coaches who filmed the games. My job during the game was to chart the offensive plays. For every play, I would have to write down these details on the form:

• Down and distance (1st and 10)
• Where the ball was placed ("our" 35 yard-line or "their" 35-yard-line)
• What part of the field the ball was placed (center, left, right, midcenter, midleft, midright)
• Our formations
• The play calls
• Pass or run (P, R)
• Result of the play (Keyes 8-yard run, Ballard 17-yard catch)
Then I would repeat that sequence for every offensive play.

During the Berea scrimmage, things seemed to be moving at hyperspeed. Through my headpiece I could hear Coach Mazur and Coach Troxler calling the plays and giving their opinions down on the sideline. Coach Stone was sitting next to me giving those guys information about Berea's defensive alignment. I was trying to write everything down as fast as I could so that I was ready for the next play. It took most of the scrimmage, but I slowly started to get the flow of the game and the frequency with which the plays were being called. And being the perfectionist that he was, Coach Stone was there to help me fill in the gaps if I missed a play or the result of a play.

The regular season hadn't even started before we experienced controversy. It came the following week. We had our last preseason scrimmage, against Lakewood's St. Edward High School. St. Ed's is a Division I private school. Massillon is a Division II public school. The differences in divisions are determined by the number of eligible male students. Coach Moore likes to schedule a bigger school for the final scrimmage to see where we needed work and how we looked against a perennially good team. With Lakewood coming off a Division I state championship win in 2018, it fit the bill.

After the starters battled it out for the first half of the scrimmage, I left the box to join the rest of the coaches along the sideline to watch the second- and third-team players take their shot. While I was on the sideline, Coach Moore walked over to me and said, "Let's get Jean-Luc in there." Jean-Luc Beasley was a junior running back who was small, but a strong runner with a lot of potential. He had come up through the youth football program in Massillon. He was one of those athletes who, if he had gone to a school other than Massillon, would have either started or split time as a starter. But in 2019, Massillon was loaded at running back. It started off with a senior transfer to Massillon from St. Vincent-St. Mary. His name was Terrance Keyes, Jr. (TK), who was five foot nine and 190 pounds. We had high hopes for what he could bring to the team. Before his transfer it was thought that senior Zion Phifer, five feet eight, two hundred pounds, would be our starter. He had spelled Jamir Thomas the previous year. Thomas just broke every record in the Massillon running back book. He had left last year as the running back with the most points, yards, and touchdowns. Zion had played behind him without much of a drop-off. With the transfer of TK, Zion found himself once again in the backup position. We also had a very good third running back in junior Raekwon Venson, who could've started anywhere else in the county, yet he was our *third-string* back, and he was hardly a third-string back at all.

The problem for Jean-Luc was that he felt like he didn't get the carries he deserved during the first two scrimmages. He didn't get that many carries against St. Ed, either, and felt this last scrimmage was the final straw. The reality, however, was that he was our fourth running back. That's not to say he wasn't talented, but we had guys in front of him who were more talented and got all the reps. So where did that leave Jean-Luc, a likable and hardworking young man? Deep on the depth chart. We tried getting Jean-Luc as much playing time as possible in the three scrimmages, but it was just tough because of our personnel. After Coach Moore gave me orders to play Jean-Luc, I went down the sideline looking for him. He was at the far end, away from the line of scrimmage. "Jean-Luc, why are you way down here?" I didn't wait for an answer. "Coach Moore wants you in right now, let's go."

"I ain't going in."

"What?"

"I ain't going in."

"What are you talking about? Coach Moore wants you in, let's GO!"

I was getting heated, but Jean-Luc wasn't budging. Jean-Luc even told his younger brother Camden, who was a sophomore running back and talented as well, to go in for him. I went back to Coach Moore and told him Jean-Luc said he wasn't going in. Coach Moore again told me to summon Jean-Luc. I walked back down to where Jean-Luc was standing, and this time, he grudgingly went in. The very next play was a running play for him. He took the handoff and ran as if he didn't even want the ball. He barely made it to the line of scrimmage, picked up a yard at best. He had a few more carries during that last part of the scrimmage, but his effort was lacking.

Jean-Luc came out of the scrimmage, as some of the younger players were getting time in the backfield, and that's when I noticed him walking down the sideline and heading to the locker room. I yelled, "Jean-Luc, where are you going? Get back here!!" He kept walking, and I kept yelling. I then started to run down the sideline toward him. Ethan Tobin, our senior defensive lineman, who wouldn't put up with any crap that brought disrespect or shame to the team, called to me, "Coach Morgan, let him go. If he doesn't want to be here, just let him go."

I let Jean-Luc go because the scrimmage was still going on. My job was to be there with the team and watch some of the younger running backs. But as soon as the scrimmage ended, I hustled into the locker room before anyone else to talk to Jean-Luc. I loved the kid, and his conduct and disrespectful attitude just weren't like him. I went straight over to him, where he was gathering stuff out of his locker. "What's wrong, man, what's going on?"

"Man, Coach Morgan, I ain't playing. I'm done. I quit."

"Jean-Luc, you worked too hard. You put in all these years of work as a little kid . . . and you're just going to give it up like this?"

"Yep, I'm done."

That was it. He took all of his stuff and walked out of the locker room. On the following Tuesday morning, which was the first day of school, Jean-Luc came to my room before school started. No one was there except me.

"Coach Morgan, you got a minute?"

"Yeah, what's up, my man?" He shook my hand and apologized for his actions at the scrimmage. I told him it was OK. I asked him if he was coming back and he said no. I knew Jean-Luc well. I had had him in my sophomore English class, and he was a good student with good grades. He was a smart young man—very likable. I watched him walk out of my classroom and down the hall of Washington High. He was throwing away not just this year, but also any chance to contribute next year as a senior. Why would he do this? I would have to wait about eight weeks to find out the answer to that question.

Photo courtesy of Tiffany Hickman-Brown

The quiet before the storm: senior players and cheerleaders strike a pose.

Front: Isaiah Roberson, Terrance Keyes Jr., Anthony Pedro, Jerron Hodges, Preston Hodges, Noah Richards, Zion Phifer, Lauren Snedeker, Lorinda Kanipe, Annabelle Roehlig, and Sydney Rice.

Back: Cole Jones, Robbie Page, Devin Hose, Lauren Brown, Aidan Longwell, Alejandro Salazar, Connor Wuske, Ahmon Williams, Manny McElroy, Corey Campbell, Peyton Mendenhall, Seth Lance, Davon Woods, and Levii McLeod.

Chapter 5
The Coaching Crew

The coaching staff I had the pleasure of working with had to be one of the most knowledgeable and talented high school staffs in Ohio. I would even go as far to say it was one of the best in the country. Jon Mazur, co-offensive coordinator and offensive line coach, had been an offensive lineman and captain for Coach Urban Meyer at Bowling Green State University and was even offered coaching positions with Meyer at Utah and Florida. The other co-offensive coordinator, Jarrett Troxler, had moved to Massillon from Georgia with his wife, a Northeast Ohio (Stow) native, and his two young boys to take the position and was instrumental in helping Massillon's offense shatter records in his first three seasons. Troxler's résumé was exemplary.

Safeties Coach Dan Hackenbracht was a former Massillon star, in the nineties, and played at Michigan State for legendary coaches George Perles and Nick Saban. "Hack" didn't mess around when it came to coaching. He was the real deal—totally old school. My first year teaching, Hack's classroom was around the corner from mine, and I would always hear old-school R & B music coming from a room. I didn't know where it was coming from until I walked around the corner and realized it was Hack's room. He was always educating the

THE MASSILLON TIGERS: 15 FOR 15

young kids on the real music they were missing out on. He never let an opportunity go by without playing some funky music for his students. From that point on, I knew Hack was a cool dude and someone I could go to for teaching advice. I never thought I would eventually coach football with him.

Meanwhile, Defensive Line Coach J. P. Simon was a stalwart at defensive tackle for the Tigers in the 2000s, then went on to play four years at the University of Cincinnati. Craig McConnell and Spencer Leno were also star players for the Tigers in the 2000s, and played college ball as well. The list of impressive coaching credentials went on and on.

Here are the coaching bios, starting at the top:

Nate Moore—Head Coach
Alma Mater—University of Dayton
Previous Head Coaching Experience—Minster High School (2010-2012), Cincinnati La Salle High School (2013-2014) (Division II state championship, 2014), Massillon Washington (2015-present) (Division II state runner-up, 2018)

Photo courtesy of Becca Moore

The Moore Family

Awards—Minster, Ohio, Division VI Coach of the Year, 2011; Minster, Miami Valley Football Coaches Association Division VI Coach of the Year, 2012; Cincinnati La Salle, state champion, Greater Catholic League South Coach of the Year, Southwest Ohio Division II Coach of the Year, all 2014

Family—Wife Becca, son Eli, daughter Ella. They have custody of Thayer Munford and Terrence Rankl.

The following is the list of the assistant coaches during the 2019 season, and Coach Moore comments about each coach.

Dan Hackenbracht—Safeties
Alma Mater—Michigan State University
Former Massillon Tiger (1990-1992)

Coach Moore on "Hack": "He's an expert that coaches our safeties and corners. I don't think anybody coaches their kids harder or has higher expectations for their kids than Coach Hack. He doesn't care if you don't start or you're a veteran, he's going to coach you hard. Everything is black and white; there is no gray area with Hack. Plus, he loves chicken. If you want to know anything about fried chicken around Stark County, Hack is the expert."

Jason Jarvis—Cornerbacks/Special Teams Coordinator
Alma Mater—University of Mount Union, Ohio
Former Massillon Tiger (1997-1999)

Coach Moore on "Jar": "Jarvis is a barrel of fun. He's an excellent coach. He does a great job as the special teams coordinator, but Jarvis is the comic relief on the staff. He just has this way about him. He should have a supporting role in one of those offbeat Will Ferrell movies like *Anchorman*. It's just his brand of humor. When we're in one of those long meetings and we're playing cards or putting together data, he hits a joke at the right spot. He brings the comic relief."

Spencer Leno—Co-defensive Coordinator/Inside Linebackers

Alma Mater—Wittenberg University, Ohio
Former Massillon Tiger (2006-2009)

Coach Moore on Spencer: "Leno is our co-defensive coordinator, and he's an up-and-comer. He's a really smart, bright guy, one of the younger guys on staff now and a guy that's getting a lot of responsibility now that he's a co-coordinator. He's very organized, superorganized, and he goes over things . . . over and over. His kids play hard for him because he's got that youthful energy where they can still feel and see a little bit of that Tiger dust falling off of him. That brings some uniqueness to the staff."

John Mazur—Co-offensive Coordinator/Offensive Line
Alma Mater—Bowling Green State University, Ohio; Nova Southeastern University, Florida

Coach Moore on "Maz": "Jon was the first really big hire for me, so he's been here the entire time I've been at Massillon. When I got hired and was trying to put together a staff, I got a text from a guy named Matt Tyler who was the offensive line coach at Fairfield High School in Ohio. He played with Mazur at Bowling Green State University. He said, 'If you're looking for an offensive coordinator, I've got your guy.' I called Jon, and we hit it off right away. We were speaking the same language in what I wanted to do offensively. We believed the same things. But the caveat was Jon and his wife both were teachers at Jackson High School [in a neighboring school district]. He was a football coach and she was the cheerleading coach, and they lived in Jackson. From a family standpoint, there were all these things that were working against him coming to Massillon."

(Coach Mazur told me that in making the decision to leave Jackson and coach at Massillon, he asked then-Ohio State Coach Urban Meyer for advice. Urban told him, "Jon, I don't know where Jackson High School is, OK? But I can drive to Massillon Washington High School blindfolded. You need to take that job.")

Craig McConnell—Co-defensive Coordinator/Outside Linebackers
Alma Mater—Walsh University, Ohio; Ashland University, Ohio
Former Massillon Tiger (1999-2003)

Coach Moore on Craig: "He's really exactly what you want as a defensive coordinator, to have all your bases covered. He is somebody that can't sleep because they're worried about this or worried about that. But it works. He's the yin to Coach Jarvis's yang, and when you put those two things together, you get great things."

Cale Miller—Wide Receivers
Alma Mater—Kent State University, Ohio

Coach Moore on Cale: "Cale is the guy that didn't take the typical route to become a position coach at Massillon, and to be honest, he's kind of like the underdog in some ways. Hack played at Michigan State, Chip Robinson played at Bowling Green, Mazur played at Bowling Green and was a captain for Urban Meyer, but Cale didn't play in college. He started coaching eighth grade here at Massillon, worked his way up to the freshmen level, and the year before I got here was his first year on varsity. He's turned into a fabulous coach and an expert at his position. I honestly think he's the best receiver coach in the state of Ohio.

Chip Robinson—Defensive Tackles
Alma Mater—Bowling Green State University, Ohio

Coach Moore on Chip: "Chip is a big guy, but he truly is a giant teddy bear. He's a really smart, intelligent guy. During the game, there are all kinds of wacky things and little intricacies that go on when it comes to the referees and rules. Chip knows that rule book better than anyone on the staff. He knows how penalties should be assessed, where the ball should be spotted, all that kind of stuff. Chip knows it all, and that's a huge advantage for us, to have a guy like Chip."

J. P. Simon—Defensive Tackles
Alma Mater—University of Cincinnati
Former Massillon Tiger (2000-2003)

Coach Moore on J. P.: "J. P. is the energy guy. He's the kid that probably ran his mouth too much, but could back it up. And in a way, he's never really had to grow up, and I mean that in a respectful way. I mean, he owns his own company, and certainly there's a lot to know with that, especially from a responsibility and maturity standpoint, but when he's at football with us he's a kid. That's who he is on the staff, and he's the energy guy that gets everybody going. He's starting to develop as a technician in his position."

Mike Stone—Fullbacks/Tight Ends/Kicking Unit
Alma Mater—Grove City College, Pennsylvania

Coach Moore on Mike: "Stone is a very cerebral guy. He's the guy that loves running data reports and will self-scout anything. Oh, and he loves the Vikings and loves wearing purple."

Danny Studer—Strength and Conditioning
Alma Mater—Northern Michigan University
Former Massillon Tiger (1997-1999)

Coach Moore on "Stu": Stu is our strength coach, and he's really one of our most important coaches because he leads our off-season workouts. That's so incredibly important to everything that we do. He's also kind of a man of contradictions, because he comes across, for lack of a better term, as an alpha male. He's the strength coach and he walks the walk. He's in at 5:30 in the morning doing heavy back squats. He's talking about being on the warpath, but he's also intellectual. Everything we do is based in science. He has all the certifications to back up his experience in the strength and conditioning worlds. He's like a college strength coach, and we're really lucky to have him."

(Coach Stu drew the section art pieces that are throughout this book.)

Jarrett Troxler—Co-offensive Coordinator/Quarterbacks
Alma Mater—Chowan College, North Carolina

Coach Moore on "Trox": "He's just a good-old country boy who happens to be a really good football coach and a great friend. He's loyal and funny. He'll tell us a little country story about Johnny Z on the peach farm or whatever and he's hilarious when he's telling them. What makes it really funny is he's not trying to be funny. He's just telling us a story, but he's got that Southern drawl, which I think is going away. It's starting to flatten out."

Dave Weber—Defensive Ends
Alma Mater—University of Akron, Ohio
Former Massillon Tiger (1981-1983)

Coach Moore on Dave: "Dave is like the uncle of the staff. He's the guy you go to for advice, the guy who gets everything back on track. Not to downplay the role he has coaching our defensive ends, but probably the most support role that he has on staff is being the guy that teaches the kids what it means to be a Tiger—especially with his weekly letters to the players and staff. Dave is the guy who lives, eats, and breathes everything Massillon. He loves Massillon football, and it's not a 'poster on the wall' kind of thing. It's everything he is, a deep understanding of everything Massillon Tiger football."

David Lee Morgan, Jr.—Running Backs
Alma Mater—Youngstown State University, Ohio

There they are, my coaching brothers, who joked with me but also taught me so much about Massillon football—football in general—and what it meant to be part of something as incredibly special as the Massillon Tiger football family. It was an exclusive fraternity that I can now say, for the rest of my life, I was a member of.

But as much as I loved my fellow coaches and how much they did for me, they were straight up ballbusters at times. Never mean-spirited, though. Never! It's just that coaching camaraderie includes getting your butt roasted. These guys could hit you with a wisecrack that would have you doubled over laughing right in the middle of the hallway, between classes, or in an important meeting in Coach Moore's office. The great thing about that is Coach Moore would be serious as hell about a formation or something related to his duty as head coach, then Coach Jarvis would say something off the cuff about Coach Moore's tone or word usage or whatever that would stop Coach Moore in his tracks, shaking his head in laughter. That was the atmosphere all the time. Don't get me wrong: when it was time to be serious, we were serious. But Coach Moore was all about humor, and allowing the different personalities to blend in with their coaching styles. When someone screwed up but it was so funny that one of the coaches couldn't help but point out the boneheaded play, by a player or coach, there was nothing you could do but laugh and forget about it.

I asked the coaches to tell me the first thoughts that came to mind when they learned that I, a guy who had virtually no experience, was now joining the big leagues—the Massillon Tigers varsity football staff—as the running backs coach. Below are their stand-up routines and roasts:

Coach Moore: "If I interviewed three thousand people for the running backs position, Coach Morgan was 2,999, with the last person probably being Bobby Boucher, from the movie *The Waterboy*, played by Adam Sandler. So in reality Coach Morgan was just a little better than Bobby Boucher."

Coach Simon: "I remember the first day when Coach Moore announced to the rest of the staff Coach Morgan would be coming on board to be the running backs coach. We were all very excited because we all knew and loved Coach Morgan and thought he would be a great addition to our staff. After the first practice, though, we had a meeting and decided someone was going to have to teach Coach Morgan the rules of football, specifically the running back position. He even dressed like a baseball guy. He walked in with the high socks and fitted hat worn down tight like a baseball coach. By the end of the season, we had him with his socks rolled down and his hat pushed up. We loved having Coach Morgan around, and we're going to miss him."

Coach Leno: "The main source of film study and playbook access in modern-day football is through Hudl, an online system that coaches and players utilize to study film, breakdowns, and playbooks. Coach Morgan, on the other hand, may have been the only modern-day coach who still used a thick three-ring binder to store his playbook. There were even rumors that when he had to watch film with the running backs for the first time, he wheeled in a cart with an old film projector. We eventually had to explain to him that he could utilize iPads, tablets, and laptops to study film with his players."

Coach Mazur: "My favorite thing about David Morgan the football coach was how he first started to come to practice looking like a scientist. Glasses, playbook, pencil, and notebook in hand, ready to pick up the offense. The first day it looked like he was in complete shock as he combed through the playbook trying to figure out the play we just ran and how to explain it to his guys. The problem is once he found the play and the rules, we were three plays ahead of him. It was about twenty minutes in when he looked at me and said, 'Damn, you guys do a lot of stuff and you do it fast.' I just chuckled and worked through the next play."

Photo by Rocky Dorsey

That's me, David Lee Morgan, Jr., smiling and Cale Miller in the background. Is he expressing the coaching staff's feelings on me joining the group? Nah.

REGULAR SEASON
(First Half)

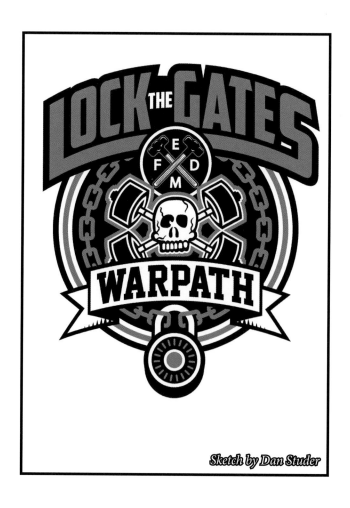

Sketch by Dan Studer

Chapter 6
Akron St. Vincent-St. Mary

Coach Dave Weber played for Massillon in the eighties alongside Chris Spielman, who went on to be an Ohio State and National Football League star. After retiring from football Spielman became an accomplished college and NFL sports broadcaster. Coach Weber wrote inspirational letters for every game to the players and coaching staff via the app Hudl. The letters would show up on everyone's devices the day of the game. After reading each letter, each week, the kids couldn't help but want to go out and play their butts off for Massillon and the community. In fact, his letters were filled with so much personal sincerity, kindness, and love for humanity that I felt they needed to be shared. Throughout the book, you will read excerpts of Coach Weber's masterful letters. Special thanks to Dave for sharing these with the team and now the world.

Coach Weber's "Words of Wisdom"

If you're going to go out on that field and think about yourself, how many touches you get, or anything that has to do with the word "you," don't put that uniform on. You don't deserve the word on your chest. I know, however, that's not

who you are. I know that is not how this group will take the
field when it is time to go. I know you will be a group that
embraces the name Massillon. I know you are a group tonight
who will allay the fears I have going into every Week 1. The
fear of losing. The fear of not being prepared. The fear of
overconfidence. The fear of not fully understanding what
this is all about, for you and for the 80 year olds pulling
themselves up the handrail to see their boys. And you are
their boys. Tonight, work your butts off for your teammates,
for your school, but most of all for the people sitting in
the stands, in a town that loves you! We know what we are,
but know not what we may be. Make your mark. Raise the bar.
Set a new standard.

    Go Tigers!! Beat St. V!!

The 2019 Massillon Tiger football team kicked off the season on August
30. The opponent was an Akron Ohio Division III private school, St.
Vincent-St. Mary. If that school sounds familiar, it's where LeBron
James went to high school. At the same time, Massillon's current
superintendent, Paul "Sal" Salvino, was a football coach. LeBron played
his freshman and sophomore seasons as a wide receiver, but his mom
Gloria was hesitant about him playing his junior year. Sal said, "There
was a knock on the football coaches' door, and there stood LeBron. He
said, 'You know I really want to play, but my mom ain't cool with it. So
can I be the water boy?'" LeBron's mom eventually let him play. But for
a while, the future NBA superstar was the water boy for St. V.

    On this night, it was a different St. V alum that was on everyone's
mind. Over the past few years this game became quite a rivalry, with the
teams splitting the wins and losses. The Tigers did win in 2018, en route
to their first undefeated season of the new century. The Tigers would
open the 2019 season with a bit of drama built in. In the 2018 game, St.
V had an all-state running back who gave the Tigers fits. His name was
Terrance Keyes. The same kid that I was now coaching. Terrance became
our first-string running back despite the fact that we had Zion Phifer
returning from last year. Zion wasn't thrilled with the new transfer.

    I had Zion in my sophomore English class, and we were close. During his junior year, he would always come to my room in-between classes or at lunch just to talk. Let's be real, a majority of kids hate English for the most part, especially African American kids. When they saw me, this man who looked like them, who authored successful books, spoke well, dressed well, but would get in their faces like their uncle, they respected and wanted that. I treated them with kindness, and toughness. So even when I didn't have them in my class anymore, they stopped in for a quick conversation or advice. Which eventually turned into a trusting, loving relationship.

One day Zion came into my class and was moping. I said, "What the heck is wrong with you, man?"

Zion was always a positive kid with a smile on his face. He said, "I heard this dude from St. V is transferring here." I could tell Zion was feeling sorry for himself. Terrance was an outstanding running back, and Zion thought he was going to lose his job. He also thought Coach Moore and the staff had lost faith in him. The reality is Coach Moore had nothing to do with Terrance's transfer. St. V had a new coach, and Terrance told me that things changed for him at that point.

Photo by David Lee Morgan, Jr.

#29 Zion Phifer stops in my classroom to show off his Tiger cleats.

Terrance's father, Terrance Keyes, Sr., explained it this way: "The head coach at the time wasn't a teacher at the school, so Terrance felt he didn't have a connection with him."

I told Zion, "Look, Coach Moore has nothing to do with this. Nobody's kicking you to the curb. Look at what you've done for us. We need you. Trust me, man, we're going to really need you this year more than ever."

Coach Moore commented, "I can see that Zion may have been hurt

47

or upset, but we obviously didn't have anything to do with whether Terrance was going to come to Massillon. It probably took Zion a little while to come to terms with it, initially."

That was the truth. Zion got over his inferiority complex relatively quickly and was ready to go by the start of the season. He was a little heavier and moved to the position of H-back, basically a fullback. What made Zion so special was that he was quick and had speed. With the extra weight, he was even harder to bring down. Zion fit into his new role nicely, and that happy-go-lucky attitude came back, and never faded after that. We played music during practices, and Zion would run a play, then go right up underneath Coach Moore's face and start dancing like he was in a club. Coach Moore would just shake his head and crack up.

While Zion had been around the Massillon program and knew what to expect, for Terrance it was quite an adjustment. St. V is a heck of a school and full of great tradition. But it isn't the same as being the lead running back at a school that gets the media attention Massillon gets.

Terrance moved to Massillon with his father in the summer of 2019. He was a high-energy young man. His smile and upbeat, positive personality preceded him. You knew he was in the room, because laughter and exuberance always poured from the shadows where he stood. St. Vincent-St. Mary fans weren't feeling the same way about Terrance by the time our opening game came around. All you needed to do was look at one of the signs aimed at him.

"I remember that banner they had," Terrance recalled. "Because my name starts with T-E-R-R they made a sign that said 'TERR Up The Tigers.' I knew there were going to be haters."

Before Terrance even registered his first official carry in that game, there was speculation from outsiders about whether he was even going to start. That was because Terrance sat out the St. Ed scrimmage with a minor toe injury he had suffered in practice a few days prior. He wasn't 100 percent for the St. Ed scrimmage, so we decided there was no reason to play him. It was best that he rested and was completely healthy for the regular-season opener against St. Vincent-St. Mary the following week. Terrance stood on the sideline and never played a down. The rumor mill was swirling, and Terrance was stirring the pot.

"I read some stuff on social media that some of my boys in Akron thought I was on the second string because they didn't see me in the St. Ed scrimmage. So I played along and just told them that [Massillon] didn't have me starting and that I was on the second team."

Terrance said the week leading up to the St. V game he stayed off social media. "I knew there was going to be a lot of distractions, and I didn't want people to hear from me. I played it smart and stayed focused until Friday. I mean, truth be told, when I transferred to Massillon there was a lot of hatred toward me from people in Akron, and from people I would've never thought would be the ones. I just prayed through that process, because my relationship with God is no accident. I just kept my mind and my mentality clear and got ready to do what I'm passionate about and what I love, which is playing football. I was humble enough to block out all of that negativity."

TIME OUT!

Senior captain and defensive nose tackle Emanuel "Manny" McElroy started the season with an amazing friendship with ten-year-old Nathan Forte. Nathan is the younger brother of our starting H-back, junior Michael Billman. Nathan was diagnosed with osteosarcoma (bone cancer) in December 2018 and had undergone numerous chemotherapy sessions at Akron Children's Hospital. Michael knew his little brother needed his spirits lifted, and he looked to his teammate. Manny and Nathan became friends during the summer before our season started. Manny would go to Michael's house to help with yard work or just to hang with Nathan. "When I first met Nathan, I didn't know how to act or what to do, because he was going through so much," Manny said. "But once I met him, we just hit it off. That's my dawg." Nathan said, "Manny is always nice to me, and he's funny."

Their relationship carried onto the field. Manny was voted one of our team captains and Nathan became our honorary captain, so he had the opportunity to walk to midfield for the coin toss at all of our home games. It was a pleasure each game to see all the football players, Massillon or the visiting team, shake hands with Nathan. He was part of the team.

"I just love Massillon football," Nathan said.

Photo courtesy of Manny McElroy

Captains and friends
Nathan Forte/Manny McElroy

Paul Brown Tiger Stadium comes alive on the opening home game of the year. The band fills the field in the formation of a large M. A thirty-foot inflatable tiger is rolled onto the field. The players come running out of a huge black tunnel as younger kids are gathered by the opening, creating parallel lines of future Tigers looking up at the heroes as they emerge. Smoke billows from the front of the tunnel. The players rock back and forth. The crowd chants "T-I-G" and answers itself with "E-R-S." The cheerleaders carry a large metal circle with paper covering for the team to burst through. Fireworks explode, and the announcer belts out, "Heeeeeeeeeeere's the Tigers."

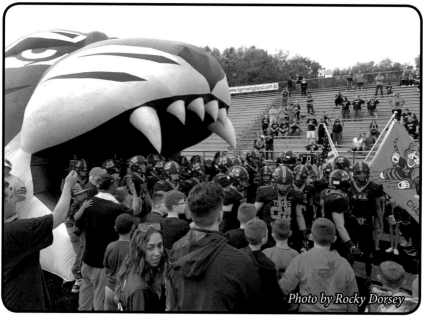

Photo by Rocky Dorsey

The players are ready to take the field.

I never got a chance to run on the field before the games because my job required me to be up in the press box with Coach Stone, Coach McConnell, and Coach Leno. Also in the box were coaches from the freshman squad: Kyle Allman, Bo Grunder, Josh Remark, Brian "Smitty" Smith, Ken Pryor, and Ed Glick. We would all head up to the press box about twenty minutes before kickoff. I would leave the locker room and walk to the bottom of the concourse to make my way to the press box. The very first section I passed was the student section, and I would hear so many students screaming, "Mr. Morgan! Hey, Mr. Morgan!" I wanted to look up and wave, but I had to be focused, in "coach mode." I had my clipboard in hand and head down. I looked up and smiled, but then looked back down quickly.

I walked to the middle of the stadium stairs and ran up the steps. I could hear friends and colleagues yelling my name, but I wouldn't look up or acknowledge anyone, not even Jill. Again, my goal was to stay focused. I wondered if they thought I was being rude, and I felt bad. I just wanted to get to the press box and get ready for the game to start and do my job. Michelle Grimes, a teacher and colleague of mine at the high school and one of the nicest ladies on the planet, saw me in school and said, "David, you never say hi to us when we call your name." She wasn't mad, but curious. I explained to her that I get myself in a zone. Michelle and her family sat at the top of the stadium—a row or two before the press box door. The very next home game, I kept my head down all the way up the stadium steps until I got to where Michelle and her family were sitting, and I made sure to look up and wave.

The buildup to the game was intense, but we came prepared and did our job, rolling to a relatively easy 44-14 win. Terrance had a decent performance, finishing with a game-high fifty-eight yards on fourteen carries, with two touchdowns. He told me afterward, "Coach, I worked so hard. I'm not really satisfied." I understood why he felt that way. He wanted one of those record-setting performances against his former team. We didn't need him to do that, and he really didn't need that either. We just needed a solid win to build on.

Terrance Keyes, Sr., wasn't surprised by his son's reaction: "Terrance is his own biggest critic, and I always told him not to be so hard on himself. I think the pressure came with him just wanting to have a standout game against his former team."

As for a record-setting performance, it did happen in that game. Not on the ground, but in the air. We were blessed with two of the best wide receivers in the state: juniors Jayden Ballard and Andrew Wilson-Lamp. Expectations were high when it came to these highly-recruited Division I college prospects. Yet no one expected a record to be broken in the first game of the season. Ballard already had an offer to go to OSU, but on this night it was Wilson-Lamp, a West Virginia recruit, who made history. He set a single-game school record with 232 receiving yards on eleven catches and one touchdown—a forty-five-yard reception. The previous record of 222 yards had been set by Austin Jasinski in 2016, also in the first game of the season. Wilson-Lamp had played the game with a heavy heart: his grandmother, Mary L. "Sista" Robinson, had passed away just the night before at age 78.

"I was with her at the hospital up until she died," Andrew said. "We were super close to each other. I was at her house every weekend and during spring breaks all the time. I was having a hard time going through school the next day, and my mom was like, 'Andrew, just keep fighting.'"

Andrew had asked to meet with Coach Miller the day of the St. V game. "[Andrew] told me about his grandmother and said, 'I don't want anybody to know. I don't need something to happen to me to be the spotlight of our first game. I just want to keep it private. I just wanna let you know I'm struggling, Coach.'"

It was a tough week for Andrew, losing someone so close. You combine that with the start of the school year and his first start at wide receiver and you had to feel for a kid like that. Andrew came out and was on fire right from the beginning.

Photo by Rocky Dorsey

Terrence Rankl lifts Andrew Wilson-Lamp, who celebrates getting into the Massillon record books. He bravely turned tragedy into triumph.

"I went into the game with the intent to just tear their secondary apart. I wanted to tear everybody up," Andrew told me. "I was just focused on my grandma. I didn't know what records I broke until after the game, and that's when I broke down with my mom. I didn't expect to do all that. That was for my grandma."

Coach Miller said, "I knew what kind of night it was going to be for Andrew. It was his first catch of the game, and our first possession, after we held St. V on its opening drive. It was one of his best catches of the year. It was a post. The ball wasn't led in front of Andrew. He had to adjust and back-shoulder catch it." The play was a fifty-one-yard reception from senior quarterback Aidan Longwell, and on the next play Terrance Keyes scored on a thirteen-yard run, giving us a quick 7-0 lead.

Miller continued, "Andrew was locked in the entire time. He wanted the ball. He wasn't boisterous or overbearing about it at all. He just wanted to go out there and perform and do whatever was asked. Jayden couldn't have been happier for Andrew. I couldn't have been happier for him. It was a special night for him, and I think it really jump-started the season for us. It was just an all-around really tough week for Andrew and [his mother] Kelly. The week ended on a high note for him. It was really a special night for Andrew and his family."

Terrance, who would experience a similar loss later in the season, said: "I was really, really, REALLY happy for Andrew. We all were. I was just so excited for him, because it takes a lot of guts and courage to go out there in front of so many people and play after you just lost your grandma. We were proud of him."

THE SCORE BOARD

Teams	Q1	Q2	Q3	Q4	F
Massillon Tigers (1-0)	7	14	16	7	44
St. Vincent-St Mary (0-1)	0	14	0	0	14

Chapter 7
Canton GlenOak

Coach Weber's "Words of Wisdom"

What I need you guys to start to understand quickly is that you're going to need more than the talent you have to get us to week 15 and win a State Championship. It's going to take the overwhelming Will of a Massillon Tiger to get through our region. Talent only puts a finishing touch on Will. Do you want to win? Yes! Do you desire to win? Hell yeah! Do you have the Will to win? We'll see. We'll see when your backs are against the wall who you are. Do I believe Massillon Will is inside of you? Yes. Do I believe we've had to pull from that Will yet? No. Do I believe that Will only shows itself in important, tight games? No. That is when we all see it because we're looking for it. Having the Will or not having it. However, Will is also evident in games like tonight, where we are clearly the better, more talented team. Mistake filled play. Lazy play. Allowing an inferior opponent to have hope. That is playing with the hopes your talent will win out. Play with determination tonight. Extinguish their

hope. Crush their will. Do what is expected of a potentially
great football team. Assert your Will.
"Men at some time are masters of their fates. The fault, dear
Brutus, is not in our stars, but in ourselves, that we are
underlings."-Julius Caesar, Shakespeare
  Go Tigers!! Beat GlenOak!!

Besides McKinley, which has been on Massillon's schedule since 1894, GlenOak is the only team in Stark County that will schedule Massillon on a regular basis. Louisville, our week-nine game, scheduled us for 2018-2019, but announced it was dropping us after that even before the 2019 season started. The other area high schools pass on playing the Tigers, despite the guarantee of high ticket sales that a game with Massillon always brings. The reasons each local school passes up the money and the chance for its students to play in front of a huge crowd are for each school to say. What this means for Massillon is that it has to bring in teams from across the state, and sometimes the country, to schedule ten games. GlenOak has scheduled Massillon for the past eleven years, and up until very recently these games had been barn burners. While geographic proximity is one reason this game is always a fun one for our players and our student body, the other is for personal connections among the coaching staff.

One of the major connections belongs to Coach Jason Jarvis. He was the cornerbacks and special teams coach at GlenOak from 2009-2013, before returning to Massillon, his alma mater. Coach Jarvis had two younger brothers on the GlenOak coaching staff as we headed into our home game against the Golden Eagles. Dustin Jarvis was the outside linebackers/special teams coach, and Kurt Jarvis was the co-defensive coordinator. Jason said he enjoyed his time coaching at GlenOak and that it made sense that GlenOak had been on our schedule for years. GlenOak's former head coach Scott Garcia coached at Massillon in 2005, when the Tigers made it to the state finals. He got the GlenOak head coaching position the following season, and started scheduling Massillon in 2009.

"They have good people over there," said Jason, who was on Garcia's staff. "Scott really respects Massillon. When he got the head coaching job at GlenOak, he wanted to put Massillon on the schedule."

Coach Moore told the Massillon paper, *The Independent*, in 2018, "[The GlenOak game] is like a league game for us. There's such an extreme there with our real rivalry, with the Massillon-McKinley game, that I think to call anything else a rivalry doesn't make any sense to me. It feels like a league game, like the St. Vincent-St. Mary game, because we play them all the time." GlenOak had a down year in 2018 and was under the direction of a new coach in 2019, Beau Balderson, making the Golden Eagles a respected underdog for this game.

Since we were counting on our first-stringers to handle the game quickly, which meant getting some playing time for the backups, this would be an interesting game that tested junior running back Raekwon Venson's will to perform. All week long I kept telling Raekwon, who

TIME OUT! Senior captain and offensive lineman Cole Jones was in my senior writing workshop. One day in class, Cole told me that he, Coach Moore, and Aidan Longwell were stopped at a light and saw an elderly lady in a parking lot starting to clear the snow off her car. Aidan and Cole got out and scraped the ice and snow off the car for her. Cole said, "She told us she was ninety-six and had Paul Brown as a teacher." I almost lost my mind.

The woman's name was Frances Butts. I asked Cole to show me on Google Images where she lived. I located her address and left school during my fifth-mod lunch. I found her residence, knocked on her door, and heard, "Just a minute." When Frances answered the door, I explained why I was there, and just like that I was face-to-face with this wonderful woman. One moment I had no idea who Frances Butts was; the next I was in her living room.

I knew my time was limited with Frances because I had to get back to school for my next class, but listening to her reminisce was like taking a ride through history.

I had to ask her, "What was it like to have Paul Brown as a teacher?"

She replied, "Well, it was 1939 and I was a junior. He was a very caring teacher. But I wasn't the greatest with dates and history . . . so I got a D with him one time. Don't tell anybody." She chuckled.

Frances proudly told me she had just recently had her driver's license renewed for another four years. "I hope I can still use it for the next four years," she joked.

was our third-string running back, to be ready. If he had gone to school anywhere else in Stark County, he would have been the No. 1 running back, or at least splitting time as a starter. But because of Terrance and Zion, Raekwon was our number three. He was a strong, solid runner with good speed, quickness, and power. I could tell Raekwon all about his positive attributes, but those were just words to him. The bottom line was he wanted to start. We all admired and respected his passion, fortitude, and tenacity. He felt that he had put in all the work and dedicated himself to the program enough to be able to start or at least share the duties. That changed when Terrance transferred. And the reality was that there was going to be competition that some of our guys didn't expect.

"I was kind of irked because I felt like the coaches didn't really have faith in me and Zion, and that they didn't trust us," Raekwon said. "Then Terrance came in, and when I saw him during one of the first workouts, he was going at it hard. It just made me want to work harder. I didn't really have anything against him, honestly, and we eventually became a lethal [running back] group."

To Raekwon's credit, there was no animosity between him, Zion, and Terrance whatsoever. Raekwon didn't like taking a backseat to our one-two punch of Terrance and Zion, but he had to wait for his moments. The GlenOak game was his moment early in the season. From day one, I had to put in Raekwon's mind that he was a very capable running back and that we were going to need him. Because we planned and hoped to go fifteen weeks, if any of our guys, God forbid, went down, he was going to have to step up. But early in the season, that wasn't his mindset, and that was an issue. It was easy for him to get off his game if he didn't feel motivated or if he felt like he wasn't getting enough carries. I had to talk to him and coach him back up. It was part of my job to get him mentally sharp and focused again.

Leading up to the GlenOak game, I told him, "Raekwon, I got a feeling for you this week, my man." I kept telling him that, every opportunity I could. We had handled a good St. Vincent-St. Mary team in week one. I knew if we came out and played the same way against GlenOak—a good team, but not as good as St. Vincent-St. Mary— Raekwon would get his opportunity. Sure enough, the game played out exactly the way we all thought it would.

We jumped out to a 27-0 lead by the end of the first quarter and took a 46-0 lead in the second quarter. Raekwon got some carries then, but most of his action came in the second half. We went into the locker room with a 55-6 halftime lead. Before we broke off for our position meetings in the locker room, I grabbed Raekwon, pulled him to the side, and said, "I told you!!!" He said, "I know!"

After our meetings and halftime "adjustments" (you don't make too many adjustments when you're up 55-6 at halftime), I was heading up to the coaches' box, and before I did I went over to Raekwon and said, "Keep doing what you're doing. This is your time, man. Keep having fun. You worked hard for it. You earned it." He responded, "Yes, sir, Coach," and had a smile, ear to ear, like a Cheshire cat. I was so proud of him. He finished with ninety-eight yards on sixteen strong carries. He did go over the one hundred-yard plateau at one point, but a rush of minus-three yards brought him down to ninety-eight. He didn't score any touchdowns, but we didn't need him to; we just needed him to run hard. "I felt like it was a game where I had to set the tone for me for the rest of the season," Raekwon said afterward. "I wanted everybody to know that we don't just have Terrance and Zion. We also have me."

Raekwon was happy and proud after the game because he had contributed, and he didn't know when he was going to get that opportunity again. I knew he would have opportunities; he just had to be ready when those opportunities came. Against GlenOak, he showed everybody in the stands that he could hold his own and that he wasn't just another third-string Massillon running back standing on the sidelines.

THE SCORE BOARD

Teams	Q1	Q2	Q3	Q4	F
Massillon Tigers (2-0)	27	28	0	0	55
Canton GlenOak (1-1)	0	6	0	7	13

Chapter 8
@Warren Harding

Coach Weber's "Words of Wisdom"

Our family is friends with the Kausnick family. They had three boys. Scott, Chad, and Brenden. Scott was older than me by five years and was the center on the 1978 team. That was an amazing McKinley game in 1978. The Tigers came back from a 10-6 deficit to win 13-10. I remember watching Scott during the game. In the first quarter of the McKinley game, Scott broke his right hand, and he was right-handed. So he switched to snapping the ball with his left hand. In the second quarter of the game, he broke his left hand and for the rest of the game snapped the ball with both hands to get it up to the quarterback. But he never left the field.

We all have opportunities in our lives to become a hero to someone, for a variety of reasons. You might think "That isn't me, I'm no one's hero." Yes, you are. Putting on that uniform makes you a hero to a large segment of our town. Become that HERO!!

　　Go Tigers!! Beat Warren!!

This game allowed me to see two of my heroes. It was also my homecoming, in every sense of the word. This was more than just another week-three game. It was us playing in my childhood backyard, in front of friends and family whom I have known my entire life. When I was growing up we lived about a five-minute drive from Mollenkopf Stadium. Before I could drive, my friends and I would walk home from school every day, right past Buena Vista Cafe. It was a neighborhood restaurant owned by a Greek family, the Frankos. Everyone knew what Buena Vista meant: Uncle Nick's Greek fried chicken. In my opinion, Uncle Nick's chicken is the best in the world.

Before I was old enough to go to the games with my dad, I would play toss-up football with myself in our big, open-field yard. We lived so close that you could sometimes hear Mr. Kraker (the longtime PA announcer, who also was my seventh-grade science teacher at Harry B. Turner Junior High School) announcing names. I would throw the ball up in the air like I was throwing myself a touchdown pass, and every once in a while I timed it just right, so that the "BOOOOOM!" from the fireworks signaling that Warren had scored would go off, and I would spike the ball and jump up and down like I scored.

It's true we were back in my home stadium, but the team we were playing really wasn't my alma mater. It was, but it wasn't. I graduated from Warren G. Harding High School on the city's east side. Our crosstown, west-side rival were the Warren Western Reserve Raiders. But in 1990, the city consolidated high schools, moving those students to my high school. Our mascot was the panther, and our colors were red, black, and white. They wore black and yellow. Since they were being uprooted, administrators decided to call the school Warren Harding but changed the team name to the Raiders, and allowed the colors to be black and gold (with some yellow). So on September 13, 2019, Massillon was playing the Warren Harding Raiders. To put that into a Massillon/McKinley perspective, think about Canton McKinley closing and those students having to enroll at Massillon. (Even hard-nosed Craig McConnell wouldn't be able to keep the fights down if that ever happened.)

People in Warren were divided over the consolidation plan, but in the end one great thing came out of it from a Warren high school football perspective. In 1990, the Warren Harding Raiders won the Division I state championship, defeating Cincinnati Princeton, and I was there, proudly cheering.

But this wasn't a state title tonight, just the eighty-second meeting of these two teams. The 2-0 Tigers were facing the 1-1 Raiders. My alma mater was, for this night, my "enemy." Outside Paul Brown Tiger Stadium, the players, coaching staff, and support staff were all loading the buses for the hour-long ride. I was just glancing at the massive banners of all the legendary Massillon coaches that hung on the outside of the home stands of the stadium. I was looking at them thinking,

Photo by Rocky Dorsey

#64 Center Cole Jones busts through the "Whip Warren" sign.

"Am I about to go home, to Mollenkopf Stadium, as the varsity running backs coach of the Massillon Tigers?" I remember all those times my dad would take me to Massillon as a kid to watch Harding play the Tigers, when I finally old enough. I felt like a kid going to Disneyland.

While we were on the bus, I made a call to my dad, David Lee Morgan, Sr. My dad's nickname is "Sonny." Everybody used to call him the unofficial mayor of Warren because he was involved in so many positive aspects of people's lives in the city. They used to joke and sing the famous Commodores song "Easy" as "Because I'm easy, easy like Sonny Morgan," instead of the actual words, "Sunday Morning." That was my dad, laid-back and mellow, all the time.

I called Sonny on the bus before we left, around four o'clock, and said, "Dad, we're about to leave the stadium here, but I need some chicken when we get to the stadium." He knew what to do.

Photo by David Lee Morgan, Jr.

My dad and me at the Warren game.

"OK, I'll have it for you at five o'clock in the parking lot under the scoreboard."

As the buses left Paul Brown Tiger Stadium, I couldn't wait to arrive in Warren. We caravaned onto Tod Avenue. I was pointing out where my relatives lived on First Street, Fourth Street, and West Market Street. When we arrived, there was my dad in the parking lot. I went over to his car and grabbed this huge box of Uncle Nick's Greek fried chicken. The players were going into the locker room to set their stuff down. The coaches walked onto the field, got the lay of the land. I walked the box of chicken over to the training table on the sideline and announced to the coaches out on the field, "Who wants Uncle Nick's Greek fried chicken?"

Guys started taking pieces. It's funny. I've never met a white guy who loved chicken as much as black people . . . until I met Coach Hack. This dude loves chicken. He eats chicken almost every day during the school year for lunch. The coaches were tearing up the chicken—two-handed grabs. Coach Mazur, who was a great, fun-loving guy, was always in game mode when we arrived at a visiting stadium. Mazur looked over at all of us with a playful smile and said, "This is bizzaro world right now. We're eating fried chicken?" He did grab a piece, though.

During pregame warm-ups, I walked over to the Warren Harding side of the field to see one of my dearest friends, mentors, and heroes, Steve Arnold. He was the head coach of the Raiders. Steve and I went to Warren G. Harding together. He was two years older than I was, but he was like a big brother and mentor to me in high school, and throughout my life. He was a great two-sport athlete at WGH (football and basketball) and played basketball at Ohio Dominican University. Seeing him and laughing and joking with him at midfield was truly a blessing, and a wonderful moment for me that brought this entire journey full circle. Interestingly, Steve and I were inducted into the

TIME OUT!

Preston Hodges, #3, was a senior captain and linebacker. Jerron Hodges, #4, was in the wide receiver rotation, and was a steady and reliable player. The Hodges brothers were a force to be reckoned with. Heck, it took me forever to realize that Preston and Jerron were twins.

Everything they did on the field was 100 percent, full speed. Games, practices, walk-throughs—it didn't matter—the intensity they possessed was unmatched. They were undersized (Preston was five feet eight, two hundred pounds; Jerron was five eight, 160 pounds), but those numbers were deceiving because they played twice their sizes. Both Hodges will attend Walsh University, a Division II school, in the fall of 2020.

They made everything a competition. In practice, Jerron would compete with his wide receiver brothers to see who would have the fewest drops, or who ran the cleanest, sharpest routes.

Preston teased me the week of the Warren game because he knew it was my alma mater. He more than teased Warren. He returned an interception forty-eight yards for a touchdown with thirty-nine seconds left before halftime, giving us a 28-7 lead. When we left the coaches' box to head to the locker room, Preston walked right over to me and said, "I told ya I was going to get your boys!"

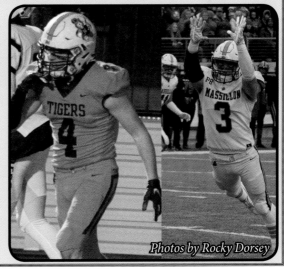

Photos by Rocky Dorsey

Warren High School Distinguished Alumni Hall of Fame the same year (2017).

The night was beautiful. The sun started to set. The temperature was eighty degrees at kickoff, and it was time to play ball. We got off to a slow start. We held Warren Harding on the opening kickoff, forcing the Raiders to punt. However, we muffed the punt, giving Warren Harding excellent field position. On their first play after the turnover, the Raiders scored on a thirty-five-yard touchdown pass, and that quick we were down 7-0. It turned out to be the Raiders' only touchdown of the game, which was great, because then I didn't have to hear my high school buddy James "Toby" Wells, who was the public address announcer and one of the best centers and defensive tackles ever to have played for the Warren G. Harding Panthers, bellow out that annoying "TOUCHDOWN RAIDERRRRRRRRRRS!" more than once. From there, we scored forty-nine unanswered points. That was the final score, 49-7. The game may not be memorable for the rest of the staff, but it will be in my memories for a lifetime.

Afterward, I met my dad, my biggest hero, on the field. My mom, who goes way beyond hero status, left at halftime. I told my dad how much I loved working with the coaches and how I loved and appreciated the chicken even more. We took a few pictures together, then I told him I loved him and had to go. He said. "You know where I'm heading?"

I said, "I know, the Buena Vista."

THE SCORE BOARD

Teams	Q1	Q2	Q3	Q4	F
Massillon Tigers (3-0)	7	21	14	7	49
Warren Harding (1-2)	7	0	0	0	7

Chapter 9
Penn-Trafford, PA

Coach Weber's "Words of Wisdom"

Be prepared to sell your body and soul against this team. Line up and punch them in the face for 48 minutes and send them back to Pennsylvania not so much understanding what Ohio football is, but what Massillon Football is.

Go Tigers!! Beat Penn-Trafford!!

Our defensive coordinator Coach McConnell is wired for every game. Not wired as in miked for a game, but wired like having consumed multiple cans of Red Bull.

He told me, "We're creatures of habit, right? So this was my routine, and it was like clockwork. Me and Coach Leno would go to Tremont Coffee around 4:00 p.m. and get a Morning Moonshine. We'd go back and sit in the office and talk about our game plan from four to five. Then, around five, I'd chug a Red Bull as I walked from the coaches' offices to the stadium. That really got me pumped up, because fans were starting to park outside and the other team would be warming up. Then, just before kickoff, I'd chug another Red Bull, and it was go time after that, baby." That was Coach McConnell's thing. We loved watching his transformation too, because it was contagious.

On September 20, 2019, we hosted Penn-Trafford, which was near Pittsburgh. They were a very talented and extremely well-coached team. It was a quality program, and the number of fans who traveled from over two hours away was impressive. Penn-Trafford came into the game at 4-0; the Tigers were 3-0. Playing a team from out of state is rough because you don't have as much film or history to study. We knew they had a huge defensive line, with weights ranging from 245-285 pounds. We weren't just waging our undefeated season, we were waging a winning streak at home that went back to October 2017. We weren't going to let anyone come into our legendary Paul Brown Tiger Stadium and have success, especially a team from out of state. No one comes into our house and sets the tone. We do that.

One of the challenges we had was *because* this team was from Pennsylvania. We had to overcome what happened the last time we played a team from that state. It was the now-classic and highly controversial Sun Valley game in 2018.

Last season, Massillon made news around the country for a new reason. On October 12, 2018, the Tigers faced Sun Valley High School, from Aston, Pennsylvania. They were a respected team, and no one could have expected what happened that night. Massillon laid 101 points on them, scoring fifty-six points in the second quarter alone. It was the most points put up by the Tigers since 1922. Massillon did all that and had only twenty-two first downs. The first string was pulled in the second quarter, but nothing could stop the scoring. We scored in just about every way possible. The score sparked articles in the Canton paper criticizing the coaching staff, and the topic was picked up nationally. You don't often see 101-6 as a football score. Now we had a team from the same state coming in, but one with a lot of talent.

With all that, every game day was loose and free in the coaches' office at the stadium. Coach Moore wants to be sure we are relaxed at that point. He said, "If your preparation is where it's supposed to be, then Friday should be fun, because 90 percent of what you're going to do has been put in place and set in motion since the winter. The hay is in the barn. There are certainly adjustments and things like that, so that when the season starts, 10 percent comes down to these tactical moves by the coaching staff and the way the kids play—how we prepared them to play. So Fridays are mostly stress free for me, because by that point we've done almost everything that we can do to win the game."

Penn-Trafford had success against us early, and it was just eating away at Coach McConnell. The Warriors opened the game with one of the best drives that anyone executed against us all year. It was a methodical masterpiece. During this lesson in time management, Penn-Trafford converted five times on third down. They put together an opening scoring drive of seventeen plays, eighty-two yards, eating up almost ten minutes of the first quarter. McConnell and Coach Leno were going berserk, and I was right next to them in the press box. The anger coming from McConnell was not the Red Bulls; it was pure Tiger rage. Penn-Trafford converted on:

- Third and four
- Third and eleven
- Third and four
- Third and one
- Third and five, resulting in a touchdown that gave them a 7-0 lead

McConnell and Coach Leno were livid.

"It didn't surprise us, because we knew going into that game that Penn-Trafford was going to be the best team we played up until that point," Leno said. "They were probably the best offensive team we saw in the regular season outside of McKinley. We knew they were a very disciplined team. We knew at some point they were going to give us their best punch, and it happened to be that first drive. We weren't going to break, and we made sure they earned every single yard that they got. That drive was a really good opening drive, but it also was a testament that our players were able to withstand that big punch."

McConnell was a madman in the first few minutes of the game. You need to know that McConnell's intense love for Massillon was deep-rooted. His grandfather was a teammate at Massillon of Paul Brown. So as a coach at Massillon, McConnell felt that each and every opponent was the enemy trying to eliminate, desecrate, and destroy the Massillon program. It was ALWAYS personal, so that opening drive was personal to McConnell.

Months later he told me, "The funny thing about all that is that after they scored, I can actually remember thinking in my head, 'There's no way they can do that every time they get the ball.' I was angry at the time, but in the back of my mind I knew they didn't have the sustainability to do that the entire game. Our kids did a great job of just settling down and focusing on what they needed to do and made the adjustments necessary."

Penn-Trafford used up so much time that it ended up leading 7-0 at the end of the first quarter—the first time we had trailed after the first period all regular season. But when you have a prolific senior quarterback like Aidan Longwell, it takes more than one perfect drive to silence a beast. We scored thirty-five points in the second quarter and cruised to a 42-21 win. In the process, Aidan set the school record for most career touchdown passes, with sixty-five. His record-setting touchdown was an eight-yard toss to Jayden Ballard. Ballard went way up in the air and just barely crossed the end zone. It was as close as you could get to just making the catch. But it broke the record and put Aidan in the Tiger history books. That night Aidan had just one incompletion. He went fourteen of fifteen for 225 yards.

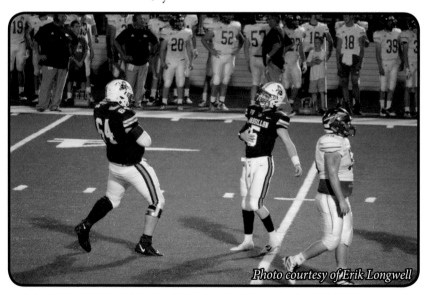

Photo courtesy of Erik Longwell

Cole Jones and Aidan Longwell rub their bellies and celebrate Aidan's record breaking 64th career touchdown.

TIME OUT! During the week of the Penn-Trafford game, word got out that a camera crew from NBC was going to be at Paul Brown Tiger Stadium to film part of our game. They were going to use the footage during the *NBC Sunday Night Football* telecast between the Los Angeles Rams and Cleveland Browns. The game was hosted in Cleveland at FirstEnergy Stadium.

That Sunday night, I watched my beloved Browns. After a commercial break, The Tigers were on screen running onto the field, with the American flag and flags of the different branches of military. NBC showed clips of Aidan handing the ball off to Terrance for a short touchdown run, the wall of fame inside our school and the plaque of former Massillon standout player John E. McVay, and a beautiful shot of the front of our stadium, focusing on the Paul Brown statue at the entrance.

NBC then went to an aerial view of FirstEnergy Stadium. Legendary sports broadcaster Al Michaels said, "Under the lights . . . Friday night, the Massillon Tigers beat Penn-Trafford 42-21 to improve to 4-0 . . . and what a history at that school. John McVay, [Ram's head coach] Sean's grandfather, former coach of the Giants and longtime GM of the 49ers, went there, and of course Paul Brown coached there for nine seasons and won four high school national championships." Then the Rams kicked off to the Browns. The entire nation, on prime-time TV, got a glimpse of the Tigers.

"Everybody was talking about [the record], and I knew it was going to happen, I just didn't know when," Aidan told me. "So for it to happen pretty early in the season was a big relief." He commented about setting the record to *The Independent* that night, "It's special, especially at Massillon. The quarterbacks and great players who have played here. I just have to give a great shout-out to my offensive line, present and past, and my receivers."

Coach Troxler was the first to congratulate Aidan. "To me, it is amazing to see a young man on the verge of greatness, of being on top at a place like Massillon, and not say one word about breaking records," Troxler said. "He never talked about it that summer or leading up to that game and that moment. He never once mentioned it. His focus was winning games. He is the most humble and talented young man I've ever coached, and now he is one of the best quarterbacks in Massillon school history."

The record Aidan broke belonged to Justin Zwick, who threw sixty-three TD passes at Massillon and went on to play quarterback for Jim Tressel at Ohio State. I covered Justin when he played for Massillon and at Ohio State. In fact, I interviewed him extensively for my book *More than a Coach: What It Means to Play for Coach, Mentor, and Friend Jim Tressel*, and he was always an upbeat, positive, humble guy. When I talked to him about Aidan breaking his record, he was genuinely happy for Aidan, even though he had never met him. "I did get to watch a few of his games," Justin said. "The first thing that jumped out is that he's a great athlete. He threw a great ball and looked the part of being a quarterback for the Massillon Tigers. The best part, though, was when I got the opportunity to talk to people who knew him, and they told me the type of person he was. All I heard was how hard of a worker he was and what a great kid he was. Those are the things that will last longer than all the records he set, even though I'm sure his records will stand for some time."

Coach Moore summed up Aidan best: "I think one of the greatest attributes of Aidan as a quarterback is that nothing rattles him. He's the same kid coming off the field whether he threw a touchdown pass or an interception. He doesn't look for the glory or the accolades or the records. He just wants to win."

THE SCORE BOARD

Teams	Q1	Q2	Q3	Q4	F
Massillon Tigers (4–0)	0	35	0	7	42
Penn–Trafford (4–1)	7	14	0	0	21

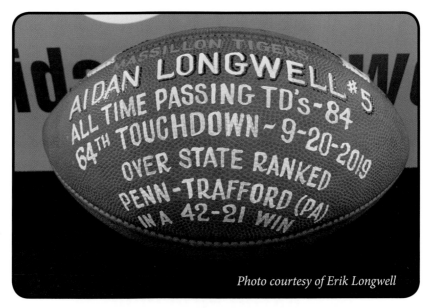

Photo courtesy of Erik Longwell

The game ball for Aidan's record-setting 64th touchdown.

Photo courtesy of Erik Longwell

Captains Aidan Longwell, Cole Jones, Preston Hodges, Manny McElroy, Ben Krichbaum prepare for the Akron Firestone game.

Chapter 10
Akron Firestone

Coach Weber's "Words of Wisdom"

Talent and hard work get you to a point, but everyone has talent and works hard. What wins that moment is the understanding that you are a Tiger and that means more than all the talent across from you. When will I stop doing this? On the day that I no longer need to do this. We're not there yet.

Go Tigers!! Beat Firestone!!

The message Coach Weber was putting out there was that although we were clearly more talented than Akron Firestone, talent alone wasn't going to be the be-all and end-all. We were still going to have to execute, stay focused, and not take Firestone lightly, even if it were 0-4. Our goal was to play like Tigers right from the start, and we did. It was almost as if Aidan wanted to get the record-setting festivities out of the way. He never liked talking about breaking records. The kid was too humble for all that. A week earlier, he had broken the school record for career touchdown passes, and heading into the Firestone game he needed just thirty-one passing yards to pass Kyle Kempt, Iowa State's star quarterback, as Massillon's all-time leading passer. Once the game started, we forced the Falcons to punt on their first possession of the game. On our first offensive play, Aidan hit Jayden for a forty-yard scoring strike. In one minute and fifty-nine seconds, Aidan etched his name in the Washington High School record books once again, with 6,056 passing yards and plenty more games to play. That is a record that may never be broken.

Photo courtesy of the Erik Longwell collection

Aidan Longwell and Coach Troxler celebrate another record broken.

Aidan shared this honor with center Cole Jones. "There are two people that touch the ball every play," Aidan said. "That's the quarterback and the center. So if the ball doesn't get snapped right or I drop the snap, the play can't happen. I never worried about the ball not being snapped to me at the right place at the right time with Cole. I knew where it was going to be. It was always the same speed and in the same spot. He was the leader of the 'Trench Life' [the offensive line] group, and he brought that entire offensive line together."

Cole's position coach felt the same way. Coach Mazur said, "Not many linemen I've coached would ask me things that made me know they understood the big picture. Cole was a great leader on the field and would help make corrections for kids before we'd even get to the sideline after a series to talk."

I asked Coach Moore if he had ever coached a kid like Aidan before, a kid who just had that something about him, that je ne sais quoi. I know I had always felt that way about Aidan, whether watching him perform on the baseball field (if you can believe it, Aidan is an even better baseball player, and was recruited by Kent State to play baseball in college), the football field, in class, and even outside a school setting.

Photos courtesy of Erik Longwell

Aidan Longwell and his family decked out in Kent State gear as Aidan signs to play baseball for the Golden Flashes. Inset picture: Aidan pitches for the Tigers.

Moore said, "Aidan has always been highly confident with himself and his abilities, and for good reason. He works so hard at it, and maybe that's where the confidence of our team came from. I think maybe people would have the tendency to say, 'Well, of course they're confident. They had a kid with a bunch of Power Five [athletic conferences] offers as teammates. I mean, why shouldn't he feel confident?' But I don't think real confidence comes from that. I think fake confidence comes from that. Real confidence comes from being prepared because of the work that you've put in. If you can mirror that with some God-given talent, you can do something special. Aidan is a microcosm of that. He's an ultratalented kid who absolutely worked his tail off. I mean, he would go from football workouts straight to the batting cages and hit two hundred balls."

Aidan explained why he signed with Kent State to play baseball: "For the most part, it was always going to be baseball. I was waiting on that right [football] offer. It just never came. Baseball has always been my first love and what I wanted to do. My goal has always been to play professional baseball, and that's what I'm working towards."

TIME OUT!

I don't know what Coach Hack ate on his way home after away games, but I know what he ate after home games. It was like clockwork. We would all be sitting in the coaches' room inside the stadium small-talking about what everyone was going to do for the night once they left the stadium. Hack was predictable. With his son Tyler, who was one of our ball boys, sitting right next to him, Hack would pull out his cell phone and make the call to Kraus' Pizza on Amherst Road, placing the same order he had placed for his family for years—pizza and chicken.

I actually called Kraus' Pizza, a locally owned pizza shop that has been in business in Massillon since 1959, to find out if they knew about Coach Hack and his eating habits. The manager at the time, a friendly lady, told me she had been there thirteen years, and everyone in the place knew exactly what Hack ordered on Friday nights after home games.

She also said the orders over the years weren't limited to Fridays!

Kraus' Pizza is a staple of Massillon football. There are deep debates about which location has the best pizza (east side versus west side). To me pizza comes from Wedgewood in Mahoning County. I never told Hack, or any of the coaches, but I had never tried Kraus' pizza. And this next part is incredible: the editor and copublisher of this book, Scott Ryan, who is also a Massillon fan, wouldn't let me sign the contract to write this book until I had a bite of Kraus' pizza. He brought in a stack of pizzas for my journalism class. The kids were horrified I had never had it. I had the pizza, loved it, and signed the contract.

FYI, Hack smelled the pizza coming down the hallway, stopped in, and stole a piece.

We led 49-0 at halftime and eventually won 56-0. Terrance carried the ball only one time, for ten yards, and Zion had just two carries for fourteen yards, which meant we were able to get a lot of our backups and younger players some much-needed reps. This was another case where I hyped up Raekwon all week and during pregame warm-ups, because I knew this was a game in which he would see considerable action.

As the guys were lined up stretching in the north end zone near our locker room, I walked over to Raekwon, bent down, patted him on his helmet, and said, "What up! You ready? You know this is another one of the games where you're gonna get to shine, right?"

He said, "I know, and I'll be ready, Coach." He was. Raekwon carried the ball eleven times for 111 yards and a touchdown. He needed that, because he definitely wasn't getting the carries he was expecting up to that point in the season. We knew he wouldn't, with our "Dynamic Duo" of Terrance and Zion burning up defenses week after week. During the Firestone game, we were able to get four other running backs some playing time: Raekwon and sophomores Nathan Depuy, Ramier Kyles, and Camden Beasley, Jean-Luc's younger brother. That was true of every position. We also gave our backup quarterbacks quality time. Junior Zach Catrone, who was Aidan's backup the past two seasons, saw extended action, along with third-string sophomore quarterback Tanner Pierce. Coach Troxler, who was co-offensive coordinator and the quarterbacks coach, loved seeing the final stats on the quarterbacks. They were a combined eight for eight. Aidan was two for two for fifty-three yards and a touchdown, Zach was five for five for thirty-one yards, and Pierce was one for one for nineteen yards and a touchdown.

No disrespect at all to Firestone, but when you play a team that you dominate early, it allows you to reward those nonstarters, those all-state scout-team players who work every day in practice to make us better. Players like sophomore Nick Hatheway, our scout team Player of the Year, who get us ready each week. They need their time in the sun, even if that time is in the last minute or two of a game. Their parents and loved ones are still there cheering on the Tigers while their child is on the sidelines. So when they get their opportunity to play, it's just as important as if our starters are out there. In games like those, it's gratifying for us coaches to see those nonstarters make a difference. To contribute to our wins. And even if a player didn't get in, he *still* contributed to our wins.

All four of my children graduated from Akron Firestone. My son Christian Morgan was a starting senior wide receiver during the 2011 season when the Falcons played at Massillon. Firestone lost 27-13, with Kyle Kempt leading the Tigers at quarterback and former Ohio State great and NFL star safety Gareon Conley leading the Tigers' defense. Christian, who played a year at Division II Ohio Dominican University, led Firestone in receptions that game (three, for twenty-nine yards) and had three kickoff returns for forty-four yards (nineteen the longest). He led Firestone with seventy-three all-purpose yards. Those numbers may not blow you away at first glance, but Massillon had a talented team that year. They had Kempt and Conley leading the way, so I was proud of the numbers my son put up in a fourteen-point loss.

THE SCORE BOARD

Teams	Q1	Q2	Q3	Q4	F
Massillon Tigers (5–0)	35	14	7	0	56
Akron Firestone (0–5)	0	0	0	0	0

Halftime

Sketch by Dan Studer

Chapter 11
Band on the Run

When you talk about Massillon Tiger football, you would be remiss if you didn't talk about the storied history of the Massillon Tiger Swing Band, which is legendary in its own right. The Tiger Band is the oldest high school band in Ohio, having started in 1914. In 1938, George "Red" Bird took over the band and started playing popular music. Incorporating dance movements, measured steps, baton-twirling majorettes, and a student dressed in real tiger skin, he created the "Greatest Show in High School Football."

Here is an oral history of the 2019 Tiger Swing Band, courtesy of Jason Neel, band director; Jenn Smithhisler, assistant director; Bob Wenzel, Tiger Swing Band announcer; Ron Prunty, band and football videographer; and four students.

Jason Neel, Director: As a band staff, along with the students who were and are part of the band, we definitely take upholding the tradition very seriously. We talk about it often—the legacy of the bands that have come before us and the legacy of George Bird in 1938, of what he started, not just in Massillon but nationally. The halftime show was invented in Massillon. We're part of that tradition. We're part of that legacy, and we work hard to carry on that legacy and tradition. For football season, we usually get started the second or third week of July, depending on the calendar. We do practice eleven months of the year. June is our one month apart. We're always playing music. Even though we're not always playing swing band music, the kids are always learning and growing as musicians, so that the next year, when seniors graduate and a new group of seniors and freshmen come in, they've improved to the level that we can carry on that tradition.

Jenn Smithhisler, Assistant Director: The Massillon Tiger Swing Band has many traditions, from our opening routine ("Fanfare," "Tiger Rag," and "Carry On") to our other school songs, like "Stand Up and Cheer" and "Eye of the Tiger," and the iconic formations we use at pregame, like spelling Tigers or ending in the big M to play the alma mater and then have the team run through it. I know that the fans love "Tiger Rag," and it still gets their heart pumping just a little faster. Seeing the iconic routines performed through the generations is something that is special and adds to the family feel and the community pride that is Massillon. It truly is the "Greatest Show in High School Football." When we say that, we are referring to the whole experience: the band performing, the team, the cheerleaders and students, and the community and fans.

The Tiger Swing Band takes the field and is displayed on the scoreboard.

Bob Wenzel, Tiger Swing Band Announcer: The expression the "Greatest Show in High School Football" does not refer to the band alone, but to the entire Massillon Tiger experience. It is the Paul Brown Tiger Stadium with its massive scoreboard, it is the team, it is the cheerleaders, it is the Village Idiots [a group of spirited students], the fans, and of course the swing band. Combine that with Lincoln Way East running through town with the orange flags from the utility poles and the game-themed signs in the storefront windows, and the entire town becomes part of the show.

Ron Prunty, Tiger Swing Band Class of 1957/Former Drum Major/ Videographer: I was highly involved in the Tiger Swing Band. I played the trumpet up to my sophomore year, then I became the drum major my junior and senior year. And I lucked out my junior year because we were invited to march in the Tournament of Roses parade in Pasadena, California, and that was such an honor. We took a train from Massillon to Chicago, then we transferred on a train called the Zephyr, and that took us all the way out to Pasadena. I even still have all the documents about who stayed where on the train, who shared a room, all of that. I do remember that Ohio State wasn't in the Rose Bowl that year, and I didn't want to go to the game because they weren't in it.

Caitlin Beckett, Class of 2021/Saxophone: Game days will always be the best part about swing band. We put in so much work and practice during the summer up until the end of the season specifically for these Friday night games. Over the years, my favorite shows have always been our first show of the season, which is always a swing show. Our very first halftime show sets up everything for the rest of the season. It shows how we're going to perform, but most importantly, it finally shows the freshmen what this band really is and what we really do. Nothing will ever match the excitement and energy of that very first game. It shows why we work so hard and what we work for.

Also, the traditions make this band so special. There are so many traditions, like marching out of the armory, a senior picked to raise and lower our band flag, and marching in to start the game, along with marching out to close out the game. But that moment when we sing the alma mater will always be the most special thing on game nights. It sets in that feeling of "this is it." Once we leave this armory, our hard work, dedication, and hearts are on that field.

Brandon Johnson, Class of 2022/Drum Major: The greatest thing about being in the Tiger Swing Band is the fans. They are priceless. Seconds before we take the field to open the show for pregame, as the crowd is chanting "T-I-G" . . . "E-R-S," the nerves and butterflies tickling in your stomach gets you pumped up, especially for me, being the drum major. When I hear the roar of that crowd, I'm ready to show off my skills!

As I'm waiting for Wenzel to announce over the speaker, "*And now, it's SHOWTIME,*" my hands start sweating, my heart beats faster and faster, but the smile on my face keeps getting bigger and bigger as I strut out to the twenty-yard line and perform a high toss. The only thing on my mind is, "I better catch this baton, for the city of Massillon." As my baton is traveling high into the air, the crowd let's out the biggest "ooh" sound until the baton hits my hand, and the crowd erupts. And then, it's officially showtime! Being the drum major at Massillon is something

Photo courtesy of Tiger Swing Band

Brandon Johnson kicks off the Tiger Swing Band.

I can't explain. It's such an honor and privilege.

To hear my name announced every Friday night is a spectacular feeling. If the fans in the stands could see the smile on my face as Mr. Wenzel says my name, they would understand what this means to me. It's like a billion dollars to me. There is only one Massillon.

Ben McArthur, Class of 2020/Obie: The greatest thing for me about being in the Massillon Tiger Swing Band was not only did I get to play an instrument for three years, I had the amazing opportunity to fulfill the position as Obie the Tiger my senior year. I would have to say this is the best part about being in the Tiger Swing Band because it brought me out of my shell, transformed me into a better leader, and led me to create new friendships.

One of the great memories I'll always have is that I was the very first person to wear a completely synthetic Obie costume. This was special to me because many people helped pay for the costume, which I very much appreciated. Another thing that made the costume unique was that it was designed by the same people that made Slider, the Cleveland Indians mascot.

Ben McArthur, the 2019 Obie the Tiger.

Katy Snodgrass, Class of 2020/Majorette: The thrill of every performance was the greatest part of being in the Massillon Tiger Swing Band. There is no way to even begin to describe the feeling of performing in front of a crowd of thousands every Friday. It's simply something you have to experience yourself to understand. What's so special about being in the Tiger Swing Band is that there is no other high school doing what we do. Not only do we perform a new show every home game, but we are also held to a high standard. Leadership, family, and discipline are values that are reinforced in us every day so we can do what we do every Friday night.

Photo courtesy of Tiger Swing Band

Majorette Katy Snodgrass at Paul Brown Tiger Stadium

REGULAR SEASON
(Second Half)

Sketch by Dan Studer

Chapter 12
@Austintown Fitch

Coach Weber's "Words of Wisdom"

Jealousy is an ugly trait. Jealousy can destroy friendships. It can make people hate others just because they can't have what someone else has. All of my life I've had to deal with jealousy because of where I am from. When Massillon was an industrial town, we were the one everyone emulated, in everything, including football. Massillon excelled at everything and others looked to us as a bar to be reached. We set the example. That's part of what drives me to get you to understand your history and responsibility to re-establish that.

Because of who you are and the jealous nature of people, there is a responsibility you have that very few others have; to be perfect. Your fans, who love you, also demand you play like they expect you to play. That is tough, but as long as you Run and Hit, and never take plays off, they will accept the outcome.

Tonight when you take that field, understand that Fitch,
like everyone else we play, is trying to place themselves in
a position as your equals. Equal with your history. Equal
with your name. They don't carry our name or our tradition.
They don't carry the weight of a town whose people's hopes
and dreams rest on what you do on Friday nights.

Go Tigers!! Beat Fitch!!!

When I was playing sports in high school, Austintown Fitch was in our league, the Steel Valley Conference, and it was a very competitive league. There was my alma mater, the Warren G. Harding Panthers, and our fiercest rival, the Warren Western Reserve Raiders, plus the Howland Tigers, the Niles Red Dragons, the Austintown Fitch Falcons, the Boardman Spartans, Youngstown Cardinal Mooney, and Youngstown Ursuline. People who knew high school sports used to argue that the Steel Valley Conference was one of the best football conferences in the state in the eighties.

Massillon's sixth game of the season was an away game in Austintown. We were entering the game at the halfway point of the regular season. We were 5-0, and we were now ranked No. 1 in the state of Ohio in Division II for the first time since 2014. But none of that was on our minds, because we were all about business. We were on a mission. Our practices were just as intense as they were during week one, and if we weren't sharp, Coach Moore would let our guys know. Against Fitch, we didn't want any type of letdown, especially coming off a 56-0 win against Firestone the previous week.

I didn't ride the bus for this trip. I had to make sure I treated the coaching staff to another Mahoning Valley staple—Wedgewood Pizza, which was minutes from Greenwood Chevrolet Austintown Falcon Stadium. I called ahead before I left school and ordered four sheets of pizza, and by the time I got to Austintown they were ready. Our buses arrived about fifteen minutes before I did, so they had had time to unload their bags and equipment in the locker room and walk to the field. I pulled up to the front of the stadium and walked over to the track with my four sheets of pizza, and the coaches just shook their heads and laughed. Then they attacked the pizza. And in Youngstown,

TIME OUT!

The Massillon Tiger Moms are the mothers of the players who made sure we were fed before games, and we were fed really well. But the Tiger Moms didn't limit their caring and giving to just our team. The week before our home game against Gateway, from Monroeville, Pennsylvania, the Tiger Moms found out that some of the Gateway parents wanted to rent a bus so that fans could make the two-hour trip to Massillon. However, they ran into a problem.

"It was posted on Gateway's social media that they had to cancel their buses because they didn't have quite enough people to fill the bus," said Tiger Mom Libby Ginther, whose son, Austin Brawley, was a fantastic special teams Tiger and wide receiver who saw extensive varsity action. "Myself and a couple other Massillon parents felt terrible that the Gateway parents couldn't come," Libby said. "They couldn't cover the remaining costs. We jumped in and ended up raising enough money to rent the bus, plus provide a meal for the trip home." Welcome to Tiger Town, where nothing stands in the way of a game.

Libby said the response was overwhelming. She posted this message on her social media: "I have people asking if they can donate to feed the parents. Well folks, we've got that covered, too! So, I talked to Coach Nate Moore and we have a new charge. If you offered to help pay to feed the Gateway parents, I'm challenging you and everyone else, to instead donate to the Massillon/McKinley drive to end hunger and help feed families right here in Stark County. I will start a PayPal Money Pool and anyone can donate. We are WAY behind where we were last year and we need help! $1 provides 7 pounds of food for a Stark County family in need. Let's do this! T-I-G!!!"

Through that effort, 5,250 pounds of food were donated for the Massillon/McKinley food fight. (Turn to the McKinley chapter to see who won.)

In 2019, Libby was named the Northeast Ohio National Football Association's "I Am a Football Mom" mother of the year.

All the Tiger Moms were so helpful and kind to us.

Wedgewood Pizza is one of the best.

Because I was so busy making sure I had the pizza for the coaches, I hadn't realized that Coach Moore changed the times on the pregame script, so all the times I wrote on the board in the locker room were five minutes off. I remember being out near midfield with Coach Moore and all the other coaches and he said, "Where are the guys? They should be out here already."

I said, "They're supposed to be out here in five minutes, right?"

He said, "No, that's the old script, from earlier today. I changed it and sent it out to you guys? Didn't you get it?"

"My bad, Coach Moore, I didn't check my e-mail before I left school. I had to leave as soon as I could to get here and pick up the pizza." He shook his head and smiled. A few minutes later, the guys came out of the locker room to get their stretching and pregame routine going. I went back into the locker room and changed all the times leading up to kickoff.

The five minutes didn't make much of a difference in the game. We scored on our first seven possessions of the first half and led 48-7 at the break en route to a 55-7 win. Terrance scored four touchdowns and rushed for 185 yards on only sixteen carries, all in the first half. Raekwon had nine carries for seventy-one yards and one score—another quality performance for him.

Photo by Rocky Dorsey

Terrance Keyes, Jr., had his breakout game in Austintown.

But for Terrance, it seemed as though this was the first time we saw him run with abandon, run without thinking, but with purpose. He was quoted in *The Independent* the following day saying, "We've got a great passing game. We just have weapons all over. I just feel like [quarterback] Aidan [Longwell], with him having all the success he's having in the passing game, I feel like it opens it up a lot for me. The running game, it's just there. I was rolling today." It seemed like this was the game in which he finally figured out the offensive scheme—how to run and where to run.

THE SCORE BOARD

Teams	Q1	Q2	Q3	Q4	F
Massillon Tigers (6-0)	20	28	0	7	55
Austintown Fitch (3-3)	7	0	0	0	7

Photo by Rocky Dorsey

Week 7

Chapter 13
Monroeville Gateway, PA

<u>Coach Weber's "Words of Wisdom"</u>

YOU ARE MASSILLON. The Gateway Gators are coming into my stadium. Into YOUR Stadium. Into YOUR town, onto the grounds of YOUR school to punch you in the face and then board the buses back home with a piece of you in their pocket. That is something that ticks me off. But I had my time to do something about it, and we did. This is your time, your night to stick out your chest and grab Gateway by the throat and beat the living hell out of each player that steps on that field to take your pride. Fill your heart with what it truly is to be a Tiger. WE ARE MASSILLON. PLAY EVERY PLAY WITH THAT IN MIND.

Go Tigers!! Beat Gateway!!!

How big is it for another team to play the Massillon Tigers? The announcement was made in the February 16 edition of the *Pittsburgh Tribune-Review*. The headline read: "Gateway football will play national power Massillon next fall." Printed eight months before the game would even take place. Gateway Gators Coach Don Holl said in the article, "We're excited about playing them. It's certainly going to be a challenge." The article talked about how each boy born in Massillon gets a football in his hospital crib and mentioned that 26,000 people watched the Tigers play in the 2018 state championship game.

Gateway was ranked number two in its division in Pennsylvania, with the Tigers still ranked No. 1 in Ohio. Gateway had won thirty-two of its last thirty-six games. Massillon had won thirty of thirty-five. Gateway had been a terror of late, out scoring its last five opponents 213-7. This game was highly anticipated by both sets of fans.

Because I was the running backs coach, I didn't have that personal, one-on-one interaction with any of the other skill-position players. At wide receiver, we had two of the best not only in the state but in the entire country in Jayden Ballard and Andrew Wilson-Lamp, who were both juniors. Jayden had already committed to Ohio State, having entertained offers from almost every top Division I football program in the country, and Andrew's Division I offers were building. Andrew eventually committed to West Virginia, later in the year.

They were coached by Cale Miller, who, in my opinion, was one of the best high school wide receiver coaches in the country, as Coach Moore already attested. Cale had one of the best relationships with his players I had ever seen. Coach Miller said, "They know I care about them, which is number one, and that's the only way I can get any of them to trust me. They know I love them all. I'll tell them if they suck that day. I'll tell them, 'You didn't play great . . . pull your head out of your ass today . . . you're awful today.' But at the same time, you have to really build their confidence. I'm not a screamer."

Those guys respected every word that came out of his mouth because he wasn't a screamer. He was very calm, cool, and collected. He spoke in a tone that let you know he trusted you, and those guys played their asses off for him. Don't get me wrong: if they screwed up, Cale was on them.

By the time we faced Gateway, Jayden had 464 total receiving yards and Andrew was just behind with 417, so it showed how equally productive they were as a tandem. Andrew had put himself in the

Massillon record books in the first game of the season. It was only a matter of time before Jayden put his name in the books as well. It came against Gateway, a game we wound up winning 48-12.

Photo by Rocky Dorsey

Jayden Ballard strolls into the end zone and the record books.

With about six minutes left in the second quarter, we started our drive at our own four-yard line, thanks to a fumble recovery by senior linebacker and captain Ben Krichbaum. On first down we gave the ball to Zion, who picked up one yard. Facing second and nine, Aidan dropped back to pass and was standing in the back of our end zone when he unleashed a perfect strike. Jayden caught the ball around our forty—a razor-sharp pass of over forty yards by Aidan—and ran sixty more yards down the right sideline (the home side.) With that catch, Jayden set the record for the longest pass reception in school history, ninety-five yards. Another game, another record set. Jayden finished with five catches for 145 yards.

Terrance picked up right where he left off at the Austintown Fitch win the week before. It seemed like Terrance was finally feeling comfortable. He finished with 142 yards on twenty-four carries and three touchdowns.

Our special teams guys, however, rarely got the credit they deserved, and this was a game where field goal kicker Alex Bauer and punter Magnus Haines deserved a lot of credit. Alex was two for two on field goal attempts (twenty-five and thirty-one yards), and Magnus had three punts totaling 138 yards, which is outstanding for a high school punter. He averaged forty-six yards a punt, and his longest was fifty-two. He had one punt that was downed inside Monroeville's twenty-yard line, giving the Gators terrible field position.

Special teams play was something Jim Tressel had always emphasized back to his YSU days. "The punt is the most important play in football," he once said in an interview with *The Blade*, a Toledo newspaper, while he was the head coach at Ohio State. "I think it's for two reasons. One is because of the amount of yardage [involved], but two is the impact if you don't do it well, if you don't protect and it's blocked for a touchdown." Tressel said the importance of the punt was nothing new, but had received considerably more attention in recent years. "The special teams have always been huge, but I just think in football it has been talked about more in the last fifteen years than it was in the first 100, and

Photo by Rocky Dorsey

C. J. Harris, Jr. and Ben Krichbaum bring down a Gator.

some of those truths now have been advertised. If you don't cover well, and they return it for a touchdown, you know, the momentum that that creates . . . and if you're just fair at your coverage, and they return it 17 yards and all of a sudden they're at midfield, that's huge. So the punt makes such a difference."

The bottom line is that if you could control special teams, you could control the game. Magnus controlled the game for us with his punts. He did a great job for us in that win.

Gateway had a lot of talent on its team. The fact that we held the Gators to just twelve points said a lot about our defense. Senior safety Luke Murphy, a six-foot-one-inch, 190-pound Kent State University recruit, had a heck of a game. He finished with five and a half tackles and an interception, and seemed to be all over the field.

"That was my best game of the year," Luke said. "They had four- and five-star athletes on their team, a four-star running back, and a really good tight end. It was definitely a fun game for me."

Coach Moore said: "Luke was a special talent for us at safety. He had speed to cover and was very physical in the run game. In our defense, that boundary safety is going to make a lot of tackles, and Luke excelled at that. He was also a quiet leader who set the standard in work ethic and balance in the classroom. He's accepted a football scholarship to Kent State, where he will be majoring in mechatronic engineering."

THE SCORE BOARD

Teams	Q1	Q2	Q3	Q4	F
Massillon Tigers (7–0)	3	17	7	21	48
Gateway (6–2)	0	6	0	6	12

TIME OUT!

I had Lauren Brown as a sophomore in my English 10 class. She is a National Honor Society member, state qualifier in the exercise science program, excelled at track and gymnastics, and a varsity cheerleader. Lauren was named the eighty-first Miss Massillonian. Winners are selected based on academic achievement, attendance, and involvement in extracurricular activities, along with a vote by fellow seniors and an essay. The long-standing tradition began in 1940.

Lauren and quarterback Aidan Longwell were a couple. Unfortunately, Lauren, her mom, Tiffany Hickman-Brown, and the rest of her family suffered a terrible tragedy when her dad, Steve Brown, passed away unexpectedly on October 11, 2019, which was the day of our homecoming game against Gateway. Lauren was on the homecoming court.

Lauren said, "That night was the crowning of homecoming queen. I realized that my dad would still want me to go and be strong. When I was announced on the field, I was introduced as the daughter of Steven and Tiffany Brown."

Tiffany Hickman-Brown added, "Lauren has been a role model for me. I had some pretty terrible days, and she pushed me to stay strong."

Lauren continued, "The only thing that keeps me and my mom going is each other. Now it's just the two of us in the house, and it's lonely without him. Losing him changed my entire outlook on life. Little things don't upset me anymore, because I know that there is someone out there who has it far worse than I do. The world doesn't stop because one terrible thing happens to a good person."

Aidan's father, Erik submitted this picture of the couple. He said, "There was lots of pain behind those smiles."

Photo courtesy of Erik Longwell

Lauren Brown & Aidan Longwell
smile on a very sad Day.

Chapter 14
@Barberton

Coach Weber's "Words of Wisdom"

Barberton is a town almost identical to ours. Back when I was your age and younger, Barberton was filled with factories. The town was filled with families who relied on those same factories. Barberton was a lot like our town and program. And at the same time the factories in Massillon started to close, so did the factories there. Since then Barberton has been a program that is good in waves that ebb and flow. They are currently on a flow. Since 2015 they are 40-7. These kids look like you. They are tough like you. The team and town will be pumped out of their minds. It is at their house. New turf. Upgraded stadium. We have to travel there.

Their coaches started out the renewal of the rivalry by not trading film until late. And only one film. Zero mutual respect from them. You are not only their season, but you are also the team that will make their program when they beat you. Yes, that is their mindset, "when they beat you."

This has to be a night when the moment your school day

```
is done, you are focused on playing to every ounce of your
ability. You have to play fast, play hard, Run, Hit, and be
disciplined. Barberton woke up today with the mindset of,
"We don't care about Massillon and their sissy indoor fancy
stadium. Multiple uniforms. They are coming to OUR house,
and we will kick their ass." Their town is jacked. Their
coaches are jacked. Their school is jacked. Their players are
jacked.

    Go Tigers!! Beat Barberton!!!
```

By the time the season began, Jean-Luc Beasley had walked off the field and quit. Many of us didn't realize what he was going through. I didn't at all. Jean-Luc was very close to his brother Chris (C. J.) Evans, who was suffering from terminal brain cancer. Jean-Luc quit because he felt guilty playing football and not being home to help his mom, Vanessa Evans, who had the responsibility of taking care of her son.

"Out of my four boys, Luc and C. J. were always the closest," Vanessa said. "C. J. was six years older than Luc. He was like C. J.'s little baby boy, so they were always really close."

Vanessa explained to me that when C. J. was twelve, doctors discovered a tumor behind his right eye, which was removed with chemo and radiation treatment. "We were told that his tumor was completely benign and that he would be fine," Vanessa said. "But three days later, results came back, and they said it was actually a stage-three anaplastic astrocytoma and we needed to start chemo and radiation again."

Stage-three astrocytoma is a rare malignant brain tumor. C. J. went into a test program, and Vanessa was informed that the original diagnosis was wrong—that what C. J. really had was low-grade glioma, slow-growing brain tumors that eventually lead to death.

Jean-Luc took the news hard.

"Luc started crying hysterically," Vanessa said. "We couldn't get him to talk. He literally went into shock."

Jean-Luc said: "It was tough the second time [the tumor came around]. I was trying to just stay positive and stay strong, but I couldn't."

C. J. died in October 2019, but before he passed away, he told Jean-Luc his only wish for him would be that he go back to the team. Jean-

Luc honored that wish. He asked to meet with Coach Moore the week of the Barberton game to talk about returning.

"Jean-Luc came to my office and told me everything he was going through," Coach Moore said. "He explained to me in a sense that if he wasn't going to be playing a lot, then he felt he should be home with his brother. It was really a completely different way to look at it. So that was what really got me thinking, 'Maybe we can find a way to get him back on the team.' It was a balance between trying to do what's best for the individual kid and doing what's best for the team."

Coach Moore said Jean-Luc wanted to rejoin the team and honor his brother's wishes. "The way Jean-Luc explained the situation to me made a lot of sense, but I told him he was going to need to explain that to his teammates, because even though the guys that he was really tight with already understood what he was going through, there were still guys on the team that think he just walked out."

Jean-Luc spoke to the team after practice one night and spilled his heart out at midfield in the indoor facility, with the players on one knee and the coaches spread out around the circle. When he finished, the players voted him back on the team. They swarmed him with hugs and welcomed him back. And with that, Jean-Luc rejoined the team, and went on to finish the year with us.

The Barberton game felt like a rivalry. The reasons for the hype were 1) Massillon was going to Barberton's home field for the first time since 1957 and 2) Barberton, as Coach Weber pointed out in his letter, had had success over the past few seasons and was thinking it was ready to pull the upset. It was a beautiful October Friday. As usual, we had a large Massillon contingent that filled up the visitors' side, long before Barberton filled up the home stands. There was a line around the stadium and down the street. Our fans always filled stands. It didn't matter how big the stadium; we were going to fill it with orange and black. We headed into this game still undefeated and still ranked No. 1 in the state. We were concerned. The week of practice was decent, not our best. We just had a feeling this game was going to be different, for whatever reason. Coach Weber always seemed prophetic with his wisdom. Barberton did everything it could to win, both by the rules and against them. We did the same. The game was penalty filled. Barberton

TIME OUT! Junior wide receiver Andrew Wilson-Lamp, senior defensive back Ahmon Williams, and senior offensive lineman Alejandro Salazar all hung up their cleats after the season and put on their dancing shoes to participate in a popular event called Touchdowns and Tutus. It was a fundraising event for the Canton Ballet, which featured twelve ballet dancers paired with area high school football players. NFL Hall Of Famer Walter Jones was one of the celebrity judges. The kids work so hard on these events.

I have to say I was proud to be involved. Ashley Bettis, who works for the Canton Ballet, contacted me several years ago and asked if I could find some players who would participate. I obliged. Over the last three years, we've had several of our players dancing on stage. Alejandro and his partner, Morgan Lineweaver, won the event.

Coach Moore, interviewed in the Canton *Repository* about the event, said, "If we can use football, which is so important to Stark County and all the communities in this area, if we can use that to help raise money for something as important as the arts, I think that's a great thing and something we're happy to be a part of."

America's Got Talent was on hand for the event and picked some of the participants to be on the show in the fall of 2020. Let's hope that some of the Tiger players can show off their dance moves as well as their football skills.

had thirteen penalties for 102 yards, and we finished with ten penalties for 138 yards. Ugly. Simply ugly. At one point, Coach Moore called for the entire team to huddle up on the field, to tell everyone to put a stop to the personal fouls and mental mistakes.

If penalties were the downside, Terrance's display of greatness as a running back was a bright spot. He rushed thirty times for 255 yards and five touchdowns. His longest run was sixty-two yards. He was phenomenal. Think of the durability and strength that a high school player needs to possess to carry the ball thirty times and NOT have a negative yard. Terrance did that. In his last three games, Terrance had amassed 542 yards and twelve touchdowns, which was quite a turnaround from the first few weeks of the season. Wide receiver Jayden Ballad had a great game as well. He had six catches for 102 yards and two touchdowns. They seemed to come just as we needed his big-play acumen. Barberton felt like it could play with us, and it did for a while. As a matter of fact, the score was 28-16 at halftime, but we outscored the Magics 21-8 in the second half to put the game away.

THE SCORE BOARD

Teams	Q1	Q2	Q3	Q4	F
Massillon Tigers (8-0)	7	21	7	14	49
Barberton (6-2)	3	13	0	8	24

Photo by Rocky Dorsey

Manny McElroy sat out the Barberton game to heal up for the rest of the season.

Chapter 15
Louisville Leopards

Coach Weber's "Words of Wisdom"

Week 9 along with Week 11 are the two hardest weeks of the season. Because of what occurs in Week 10. Last week we let Barberton mess with our heads because, for a while, things weren't easy. I wonder looking back, did the foolishness on our part stop because something in our heads clicked and we woke up or was it simply because things started to go our way? It makes a difference. If it is the latter, that is a problem, because things won't always go our way. As we move to the later phases of our season, and the opponents match our talent, maturity and focus will become paramount to our success, or failure.

This Louisville team is very talented. They will do things tonight that give us a hard time. I will be watching how we react to those situations. With our mouths or with our brains and training? Tonight is the end of season one. We play nine games in season one, and we are 8-0. If you think for one second that Louisville earned respect for you last year, I'm here to tell you, they did not. They and their

```
coaches have circled this game and have been very social
media vocal about their lack of respect for you. They WILL
come in tonight and chirp at you. Players and coaches.
     Go Tigers!! Beat Louisville!!!
```

The Louisville game was the game leading up to the McKinley game. In Massillon the season is viewed as three different seasons. Season one is games one through nine. Season two is McKinley, and season three is the playoffs. So our regular season was an unofficial nine-week process, because McKinley Week is something entirely different from anything any high school football player not from those two teams can or will ever experience. With that said, we obviously didn't want to look ahead. We had to stay focused on beating Louisville at home, because everyone remembered what happened at Louisville the previous year.

"We played Louisville in week nine, and we know what week ten is: it's McKinley Week," Coach Jarvis said. "Week nine and week eleven have always been tough for us because we're looking toward the McKinley game, which is human nature, or we are coming down from McKinley. Last year when Louisville came onto the field just before kickoff and ran one hundred yards down into the end zone where we were standing and got in our faces, it was over. Our kids put it in their minds to take it to another level. It was a bloodbath after that. Week nine was a chance for Louisville to catch us sleeping, but the worst thing they could've done was start trash-talking before the game like they did. The only chance they had—the only chance they had—to beat us or even make it close was if we were looking ahead at McKinley."

Despite the Louisville team charging Massillon and its players getting so close to ours that helmets were touching, Massillon didn't react or make a move. Not one of our players reacted to the aggression. The referees didn't call a penalty and didn't try to separate the teams until the Massillon coaches started to stand in the middle. (You can watch this happen at the 2:30 mark on YouTube on the WHS-TV channel.) Of course, this was all a year ago. What was the reaction from the 2018 team? Massillon jumped out to a 34-0 lead at halftime and

Photo courtesy of WHS-TV

In 2018, Louisville charges the Tiger team before the game starts.

eventually won 41-0. Louisville finished with only 151 total offensive yards and averaged just 2.8 yards a play. That was last year. This was a new year. And we couldn't help worrying about this team after watching the film of Barberton from the previous week. Barberton had been able to provoke us into committing personal fouls. It was likely that Louisville was going to try to do the same. Coach Weber made it the subject of his letter, but would it be enough?

Louisville ranked third all time in wins in Stark County, with next week's opponent, McKinley, at number two and Massillon at the top. Its quarterback had the school's all-time passing record; so did ours. Louisville hadn't scored a point on us last year, and this would be the last time these teams would play. We had our No. 1 ranking, our undefeated season, plus our at-home-win-streak record of nineteen games on the line—AND it was week nine. Was that enough to motivate us for what we considered our final game of the regular season?

Louisville had a great game plan. We finished the first quarter in a scoreless battle. The only other team that had held us to a scoreless first quarter was Penn-Trafford, but we had rectified that in the second quarter. Against Louisville, not so much: we went into halftime up 7-0. We were letting the Leopards, who were playing a hell of a game, stay close.

TIME OUT!

On ESPN's *College GameDay* on December 14, 2019, Army played Navy at Lincoln Financial Field in Philadelphia.

The camera had a tight shot of the three individuals on the stage, and in that tight shot was a Massillon flag with our mascot, Obie, on it. Someone was holding that flag on a pole, waving it around vigorously, but I didn't know who it was.

I quickly paused my TV, grabbed my phone, and took a picture, then sent it out on social media, asking if anyone knew who it was.

I got a response saying it was David Vasquez, a Massillon graduate who had played freshman football for the Tigers before an injury sidelined him for the remainder of high school. He had joined the military after school.

I searched for David on Facebook and sent him a private message with my phone number. He called me back minutes later, and we arranged to talk the following Monday.

He told me he had served in the Army, and one of his dreams was to attend the Army-Navy game and to get the Obie flag on national television. He did more than that. After a commercial break, there was an even tighter shot. David's face was front and center on TV, and he was wearing an orange-and-black Obie winter cap.

David told me, "I had a couple, I believe they were from upstate New York, who recognized Obie and the flag, and they said, 'Hey, is that the Massillon in Ohio?' I said, 'Yes.' Then they said, 'We know about that Massillon-McKinley game.'"

"The approach they had this year was the approach they should've had the year before," Coach Jarvis said. "This year they came to our place and didn't say a word. They didn't run their mouths like in the previous year. In terms of that, it was better on their part, because they're able to focus on the game. They read the play clock well and used it down to the very last second before they snapped the ball. That was their game plan—to use up as much of the clock as possible and to keep our offense off the field. It was a great move on their part."

We led 14-0 midway through the third quarter and faced a third-and-five situation at Louisville's forty-five. "This is such a huge play for the Massillon Tigers' offense," said the local play-by-play TV announcer, and he was right. Louisville was still in the game, no doubt.

Photo by Rocky Dorsey

Students sing the alma mater: "Through the long, LONG years. We're true to thee."

Quarterback Aidan Longwell dropped back to pass and was body-slammed to the turf on his right shoulder by Louisville defensive end Jason Goard. Aidan remained on the field for several minutes before eventually being escorted off. He didn't return.

After the season, Aidan explained the toughness it takes to be a starting quarterback: "I think people feel all quarterbacks are soft. We can't be soft. We have to be tough. Because we're getting hit sometimes with no protection, and you can't brace yourself. You're getting drilled in the ribs while you're throwing passes, so you've got to be one of the toughest dudes on the field when you're playing."

Junior backup quarterback Zach Catrone came in and played the rest of the game and did a solid job.

Coach Troxler said, "I had zero hesitation in putting Zach in. Not only did I believe in him from his daily grind, but he did it before on a huge stage as a tenth grader. In the 2018 playoffs, Aidan got hurt in the first quarter. Zach went in, and not only got us through the game, but went out there and made plays! So there was no doubt he was ready."

"When Aidan went down, we were ahead 14-0 and it was still a game," Zach said. "There were some butterflies, just a little, but it was nothing major, because I knew I was ready to play with the big cats. I just went out and trusted my skills."

Catrone was 2-of-4 for thirty-three yards, including a twenty-two-yard touchdown pass to Andre Wilson-Lamp late in the fourth quarter for the final score of the game.

We won 24-0, with Terrance Keyes (twenty-six rushes for 157 yards and two touchdowns) and Zion Phifer (seventy-eight yards on fourteen carries) leading the way.

Coach Jarvis gave Louisville credit for a good game. That was true, but it wouldn't have been a Louisville/Massillon game without your fair share of penalties, including numerous personal fouls called on both teams. We finished with a disgraceful twelve penalties for 102 yards. Louisville finished with ten penalties for seventy-five yards.

When a week-nine game ends, McKinley Week immediately begins. As the game clock ticked down to the final seconds of the game, the scoreboard says "Beat McKinley," and signs are tossed off the top roof of Paul Brown Tiger Stadium. Banners start pouring down on fans like orange and black rain drops. The team gathered at midfield for push-ups. We had just gotten out of our first real battle of the season. When everyone got to push-ups nine and ten, all I could think about was that I was 0-3 against McKinley. I needed to get that win, but the nerves were starting to build. Twenty-four points was our lowest total of the season so far. We'd had back-to-back weeks with a ton of penalties. Now we were seven days away from the biggest game of the year, and our record-setting quarterback was in the locker room nursing a bad shoulder injury.

THE SCORE BOARD

Teams	Q1	Q2	Q3	Q4	F
Massillon Tigers (9-0)	0	7	7	10	24
Louisville (6-2)	0	0	0	0	0

Chapter 16
@ Canton McKinley

<u>Part 1: The War of 1894</u>

In November 1894 (that is not a typo), Canton beat Massillon 16-6 in a football game, and one of the world's oldest football rivalries was born. Kickoffs, touchdowns, and a lot of smack talk has occurred in the following 125 years and the 130 games that have been played in that time. For perspective, the OSU-Michigan game has taken place only 116 times. Winning a Massillon-McKinley game gets you two precious bounties: 1) bragging rights for a year and 2) the victory bell. The bell is passed back and forth between the teams, and the base is decorated by the victor.

Bragging rights are even better. Are you going to the grocery store, bank, or restaurant? Well, should you see a patron wearing the losing team's colors, you are free to remind them that they lost last year. Both cities' mayors place a bet on the outcome. The schools hold a food drive and a blood drive and compete at every level. Massillon-McKinley Week is a high school football week like no other, and I experienced it firsthand as a coach. This game is so big that our pep club starts making signs in July just for this game. Every inch of space in Washington High School is covered with signs created by students. The school is plastered from head to toe with orange and black. With so many events leading up to the game, it was amazing that our staff and players were able to stay focused on the biggest and most recognizable high school football rivalry in the country. The intensity started the moment after the Louisville win.

To understand why it matters so much today, you have to start at the beginning.

Writing for the website massillontigers.com, Don Engelhardt provided this history lesson on how the legendary rivalry started, which involves two of the biggest names in football history: Knute Rockne and Jim Thorpe.

"Oddly, the Massillon-McKinley rivalry has its roots in commerce, not sports. In the 1800s the Ohio-Erie Canal, used to transport farm goods and commodities to market, was routed through the center of Massillon and thus the town became the hub for commercial activity in Stark County. But several years later the railroad had replaced the canals and due to some deep pockets in Canton, the tracks were led there. Suddenly, Canton became the hub and eventually the county seat. The rivalry then moved to sports, when each town entered the professional football arena, competing as the Tigers from Massillon (1903-1919) and the Bulldogs from Canton (1905-1919). Such was the intensity of the competition that in order to gain an edge Massillon's team 'raided' the pro team from Akron for players and also signed Notre Dame's head football coach, Knute Rockne."

The website also added these quotes about the rivalry:

"For our communities to be part of what I call the most relevant high school sporting event in our country, that is really special," said former Canton McKinley quarterback and current New England Patriots Offensive Coordinator Josh McDaniels.

"I'm not exaggerating when I say the game, to me, was as big as the Ohio-State Michigan game or an NFL championship game," remarked

Chris Spielman, who played football for Massillon, Ohio State, and the Detroit Lions. "The rivalry took on even more meaning for me because I was from Canton, but I went to Massillon."

Part 2: The Prelude

Even if you can imagine coaching or playing in a big game, you just can't comprehend the pomp and circumstance that surrounds this week. Not only do the coaches have to game-plan for what is always the toughest game of the year, but they also have to show up to a ton of events. The players don't have to just concentrate on preparing for the game and being ready for whatever wrinkles the other team has planned, they also have to keep all the activities in check. These are just teenagers. That is a tall task to ask of someone who is riding in a parade through downtown as people are screaming his name.

There are so many events planned for Massillon fans during that week. More than fifteen events, all highly attended, and each of which means the world to whatever group is staging it. One of the people who attends almost every event is Becca Moore, Head Coach Nate Moore's wife. Becca works at the school and is the first lady of Massillon, not *just* during McKinley week. I asked her to comment on each event and what it means to her. Nate and Becca have adopted two players: Thayer Munford, who now starts for the Ohio State Buckeyes, and Terrence Rankl, who is still at Massillon. Becca also set up a study group to help the players learn how to take the ACT to improve their scores and give them a better chance at playing college ball. Nate explained the influence Becca has on the team.

"She's a person that the guys can lean on when they need things. With Thayer and Terrence in the family, we'll have guys come over to the house that are their friends, and there is that opportunity of interaction where they'll come over for dinner, shoot baskets, or whatever. Those informal interactions mean a lot. And Becca is as authentic of a person as you'll ever meet. Once they realize that's who she is, not only do they respect her, but I think they're drawn to her once they figure that out."

"Authentic" is the perfect description for Becca Moore. Here she provides an inside look at one week of her life.

McKinley Week
by Becca Moore

Monday
11:30 a.m.—Hall of Fame Luncheon

This luncheon was added a few years ago and is something I really enjoy attending with Coach Moore. What makes this luncheon so special? Well, it's a sea of orange and black and red and black. Everyone is packed in for lunch, which is held in Canton at Tozzi's on 12th. When we walk in they always have Coach Moore and me go to the back so he can do his customary handshakes and pictures with the respected mayors of both cities. The first year we went was a little overwhelming, because you have to walk through these tables filled with fans (some friendly, some not so much) and go to a stage set up in the front of the room so everyone can see you. I am always looking around to see if someone is taking a picture of me eating, since I have been subjected to memes being made of me since I've arrived in Massillon. After the first year, I took this lunch in stride, stopping to pause and talk to fans and friendly faces. I always make sure Coach Moore and I coordinate. We wear our best orange and black, and of course I have to wear my signature tiger stiletto heels. This lunch is special because it gives the coaches a chance

The famous Becca Moore tiger shoes

111

Photo courtesy of Becca Moore

Head Coach Nate Moore and his wife, Becca. Nate shows off
his specially made Massillon Tiger suit jacket.

to relax and brag about what their athletes are doing off the field. I love watching all the fans' reactions when Coach Moore talks about ACT scores, overall GPA scores, and giving back to the community. I was especially grateful when Coach Marcus Wattley of McKinley spoke of his respect for Coach Moore and his program, while still being sure that McKinley was going to beat us this year.

This really is the least stressful get-together of the two teams the whole week. It is here where you hear stories of games past and you see the joy this game brings to the two communities. I sit and look out at the faces and am in awe that we really get to be part of something that is so much bigger than words can ever justify. It's the experience. The tradition. It's the anticipation you see on everyone's face. You could hear a pin drop as each coach talks. This is what a rivalry is about. A respect from both communities, yet both hoping they have the bragging rights for the next year. It makes me smile to think about looking out at the fans' faces.

7:00 p.m.—Booster Club Meeting

This is probably the most popular booster club meeting of the season. Coach Moore walks into the auditorium, as does the band, which performs to kick off the event. What I love about this meeting is that each senior stands up and recounts a memory from this rivalry or talks about why he loves being a Tiger. It is really hard as a head coach's wife not to tear up and fill up with pride when you have invested so much time into this senior class. It's something your heart just feels. As they finish their memory, they always say, "Beat McKinley and ring the victory bell." The bell gets me every time. I almost always shed a tear knowing how important this game is to that senior and that it may be the last time we see them play in Paul Brown Tiger Stadium.

Tuesday
8:00 a.m. to 2:00 p.m.—Blood Drive

I don't give blood, because I am unable to, and let's be honest: the sight of a needle just makes me pass out. I do, however, go over and thank those who are participating and make sure Coach Moore has done his part.

11:30 a.m.—Touchdown Club

Touchdown club is held every Tuesday at the The Fraternal Order of Eagles. I absolutely love this lunch. During McKinley Week there is definitely more excitement and story swapping going on during the lunch than normal. Videographer Ron Prunty is always there filming and also sometimes pulls out old films to watch and get people excited. This touchdown club meeting is run pretty much as usual, except you see a lot more "Beat McKinley" or "Pound the Pups" shirts. Two of the team captains come in and talk about the game review of the week before and the plan for beating McKinley. After our first year in Massillon, Coach Moore and I decided against sitting at the front table. Each week we move around and sit at different tables. I love this, because it helps us really get to know the fans, hear their stories, and make a connection. I think those who attend really like this too, as a different captain comes each week, and they also rotate where they sit. Connecting with the community is a big part of making this week memorable each year.

Wednesday
7:00 a.m.—Massillon/McKinley Prayer Breakfast, Canton Baptist Temple

I'm going to be honest. I have a really hard time with this breakfast. There is a lot going on this week, and this is really early for the players and our family to get on the bus and attend. The first time we attended this breakfast I felt like it was a hostile environment. The people serving from the church were nice, don't get me wrong. You walk in and the tables are set up. Massillon on one side, McKinley on the other. Both cities' mayors, superintendents, sheriffs, and guest speakers sit at the front table, looking out at everyone. Players from each team are so close that words are exchanged, and it gets intense. The coaches have to walk around and get everyone focused. Now, this is my opinion, but I feel that if you really want to come together and hold a prayer breakfast, why don't you mix the players? Why do you have them divided? It's a prayer breakfast. I honestly really don't understand this part of the week. It is just very intense, and I am always happy when we leave because I feel like we got out of there without any incident.

Thursday
8:30 a.m.—Cheerleaders Visit Elementary Schools

Photo courtesy of Massillon Cheerleaders

The 2019 Massillon Cheerleaders

I want to first say how much I love our cheerleaders! They are always smiling and are so creative. Watching the kids file into the gym at our different elementary schools wearing their Tiger gear and screaming "T-I-G" and others responding "E-R-S" is such an experience. These kids sparkle and shine and are just so thrilled to be a part of this storied tradition. I have to say that listening to the senior cheerleaders share their stories with these young students is so bittersweet. And these cheerleaders flip, cheer, dance, and yell their hearts out as if they are at a high school pep rally. They give these little Tigers a pep rally they will never forget.

6:00 to 8:00 p.m.—Washington High School Open House

Our first year in Massillon, I think I walked around with my jaw on the floor for the first open house. I have never in my life seen anything like this. From the moment you walk through the entrance of the high school it is covered with spirit posters ceiling to floor. I mean ceiling to floor. The senior pictures are taped to the floor going up the stairs. There are balloons and streamers everywhere. The attention to detail is second to none. Some of the posters are so detailed that you know someone spent hours making them, even though they will be torn down on Saturday. Then there are the posters that make you just laugh out loud. I have to say some of our pep club members are pretty clever. Honestly, I can't even put this into words. I think you should come and walk through and experience it for yourself.

6:00 p.m.—Freshman Massillon/McKinley Football Game

Coach Moore usually stands on the sidelines with his arms crossed looking intently at the field as if he is dissecting each and every play in his mind. I usually sit in the corner in the stands with one of our children, Ella or Eli, and just watch. This is the future of Massillon versus McKinley, and the freshman crowd can be just as loud and intense as the varsity group on Saturday afternoon. I've learned that everyone wants to be undefeated when it comes to playing McKinley, from freshman year to senior year. If the game is close you can catch me pacing at the top of our stands.

7:00 p.m.—Band Concert

Our band is unbelievable. I mean honestly second to none. The directors take a lot of time and pride in this concert, and the band really shines on this night. I don't always get to take in the whole concert, but I enjoy a couple songs. I usually stand over by the locker room gym doors so I can really take it in.

Friday
7:00 to 9:00 a.m.—Washington High School Officials,
Cheerleaders, and Tiger Swing Band at Dunkin' for Food Drive
with the Canton radio station WHBC

If you want to see competitiveness in two communities, here is where you will find it. The blood drive and the food drive are so much fun, seeing the communities go back and forth. What I love about this is that they are helping others in the community while competing. They announce the winner between quarters at the game on Saturday. Massillon hadn't won the food drive in a while, and when we wound up beating McKinley in both, the stadium exploded like a volcano. I think about all the hard work that goes into this food drive and the blood drive for both communities. Everyone on both sides should be very proud.

8:00 a.m.—Tiger Swing Band Parades through Massillon

Can you believe a judge allows the band to parade through his courtroom? I literally couldn't believe it when I saw this the first time. I was laughing and in awe. Could you imagine if you are in the courtroom and this happens? All this fun and then you get sentenced to jail as the band parades out playing "Tiger Rag"? Ha! I am in awe of how they go all day parading in and out of restaurants, businesses, and offices! No one blinks an eye; they are smiling and cheering and going crazy. This really is something so fun to experience. Because we have lived downtown for the last three years we can hear them start before we even leave for work. It is just so amazing!

10:00 a.m.—Cheerleaders Visit JRC Adult Day Center

I am not part of this, but I don't know how the cheerleaders still have voices.

11:30 a.m.—Rotary Lunch at St. Haralambos Greek Church

Every other year the rotary lunch switches between being hosted in Massillon or Canton. I only attend when it is in Massillon, because believe or not I am still working during this week. This lunch is quite exciting. The Tiger Swing Band comes in and plays, and all the seniors get up and address those attending the lunch. McKinley also brings its seniors. The cities' mayors have a bet going and always put on a show. In Massillon we always have great speakers, such as Jim Tressel (former OSU head coach) or Ellery Moore (former Tiger and local radio announcer).

1:15 p.m.—Beat McKinley Rally, WHS gym

Can we talk about how this is the most exciting pep rally in the state? I take that back: in the nation! I have never experienced something like this. The cheerleading coach and the cheerleaders have this rally so packed and keep it moving so well those forty-five minutes flies by. I literally feel after this pep rally that I could run through a brick wall. I never laugh harder than at these pep rallies. The Tiger Senior Moms do a dance, and let me tell you, they bring it every year. The step team brings down the house; the Village Idiots, a group of students who dress up for each game, compete in some crazy, off-the-wall competitions on the gym floor; the band is moving and shaking; the freshmen, sophomore, juniors, and seniors are competing and yelling across the court to win the spirit stick! It is absolute controlled chaos. The seniors are honored, the captains say a few words, and of course Coach Moore gets out there and says something, and you might as well drop the mic and walk away because the roof is about to blow off this gym. It is the most insane and best experience. I can't wait for this time each year, because the cheerleaders and coaches always outdo themselves. This here makes me feel like I am literally living out the TV show *Friday Night Lights*.

5:30 p.m.—Team Meal

Honestly, I don't know how he does it; he amazes me. I watch as Coach Moore brings the guys down and focuses them, and we have a meal. There is a little chatter here and there, but for the most part it is focus, eat, picture what you want to achieve come tomorrow. I think this is one of the most important meals. One, because we know the players are going to eat well the night before a game, and two, it reminds them, "Yes, this week has been fun, but we have one job and that is to win." I don't talk much at this dinner. I just watch and take in the faces and body language.

7:00 p.m.—Beat McKinley Parade Followed by Bonfire at Massillon Rec Center

I love, love, love the parade. Our first year here we started in the car. I couldn't believe all the people out (which, from what I know now, wasn't even very many our first year). I looked at Coach Moore and I said, "Why are we riding in a car? We have to get out and walk. We can't really wave and interact with people if we are sitting here throwing candy. I want to feel the excitement, really see it up close. I want to see their faces. I want them to know we are all in." I made Rollie, our driver, stop and let me out, so of course Coach Moore had to get out. So every year now we walk. I love it because I can hug people, scream "T-I-G," and have people yell back "E-R-S." It just warms my heart. We may not be from here, but I feel so connected when we walk down Lincoln Way, and I want to win just as much as that person who was born and raised here.

Saturday
8:15 a.m.—Team Breakfast

We were at the Eagles for the team breakfast, and it never disappoints. Everyone files off the bus, and they all know Coach Moore means business. There is no talking, just focus. You can see it on everyone's faces. The seniors go first, then juniors, sophomores, and freshmen, and then Coach Moore will yell, "Seconds!" I only ever see linemen go up for seconds. The boys are focused; they are ready. We make a quick stop after breakfast for meditation or prayer. I love this time because each player closes his eyes, and you can feel the energy and anticipation building. This is the moment. From the time they were little Tigers watching the cheerleaders to the moment they stepped on the field as a varsity football player—all that preparation was for this moment, and they are not going to back down.

2:00 p.m.—Massillon vs. McKinley

Oh, and let's not forget, you know, The Game. So I've sat in the box at the Tom Benson Hall of Fame Stadium in 2017 and almost bit my fingers off as Aidan Longwell led us to a one-point win over McKinley. I'm pretty sure I cried. I've stood on the field watching Nate raise the American Rivalry trophy and watched my aging father smile with pride, and it's brought tears to my eyes. I've gotten off the bus coming from the Hall of Fame after a win and been hugged, kissed, recorded, pictures flashing, and cried. I cry tears of joy and pride. It's these moments that you realize what this game means and what this week means to this town. It's a tradition, it's a legacy, it's a must. To win this game you have to be willing to celebrate that win in that moment and be able to move on to the next. Be ready to condition, train, and strengthen yourself mentally, for this moment will be back before you know it. If you don't, the experience of the week will be one of the biggest letdowns you have ever felt. And I for one do not want to feel that for a year.

***

Part 3: Pregame

The morning of the McKinley game was indescribable. I couldn't sleep all night and got up around 3:30 a.m. I just couldn't sleep. D. J., who had grown so much since all this started, looked at me and went back to sleep. I sat up thinking about what this would mean if we could win. I was anxious—and I was an adult. I can't imagine the pressure that was on the kids. I waited it out until it was time to report to Paul Brown Tiger Stadium. This was part of the morning timeline:

- 7:28 a.m.—On my third cup of coffee—two from Starbucks, the third from Dunkin'!
- 7:53 a.m.—Treatment for my knee. (Yes, I had our trainer wrap my bum knee. It was game day, baby.)
- 8:17 a.m.—We were all on buses headed to the Eagles Club for the annual pregame breakfast.
- 9:10 a.m.—We arrive at St. Timothy's Episcopal Church on Third Street for service.

The players sat in the front of the church and the coaching staff sat in the back. No other parishioners were there. The Reverend George Baum started leading the service, and all of a sudden I noticed a few coaches seated in the pew in front of me trying to hold in their giggles. However, one of our coaches, who will remain nameless, was trying to hold in more than just the giggles. He wasn't winning that battle and darted out of the pew and down a hallway that looked like it led to somewhere in the back of the church—possibly near the reverend's office. We did all we could to hold in our laughter. It seemed that for the one coach in question, the big breakfast at the

Photo by David Lee Morgan, Jr.

Notice the signs surrounding Reverend Baum at church.

Eagles—the biscuits with sausage and gravy, the eggs and bacon, the hash browns, the grits, the French toast and pancakes with mounds and mounds of butter and syrup, and the coffee—was congregating a bit too inauspiciously in his stomach. "I didn't think I was going to make it," he told us later. Well, he did make it, but we had to hold the buses in the parking lot of the church until we got "clearance" and our coach finally made it back to the bus. His episodes continued up until the game, during the game, and after the game.

We got back to Paul Brown Tiger Stadium just in time for me to hear a loud "BOOOOM!" I saw several gentlemen standing in the middle of center field at our baseball complex, adjacent to our indoor facility. They were in the same spot where they would typically light off fireworks during our regular-season games, only it was ten in the morning and an away game. Everyone else got off the bus and walked into the locker room. I walked over to one of the guys who was in the truck that was command central for this fireworks outfit. It was American Fireworks, based out of nearby Hudson, Ohio. The man in the truck explained to me that they started blowing off the "BOOMS!" at 8:00 a.m. and would continue every half-hour until 1:00 p.m. to "get people in Massillon pumped up."

As we loaded the buses for the short trip over to McKinley, it was relatively quiet. Everyone had earphones in, listening to whatever inspired and motivated him. I was listening to my go-to band, Steely Dan, specifically the track "Aja." It was nice and mellow. With the beautiful midmorning sunny skies, it was the perfect song. Once we got to Tom Benson Hall of Fame Stadium in Canton, the pregame atmosphere was electric. It's just 110 feet from the Pro Football Hall of Fame museum to the center of McKinley's field, which is also the site of the NFL's annual HOF game. But the location doesn't really factor in. It's The Game that matters.

Everyone seemed loose as we unloaded from the bus. It was sunny, but cold. That didn't stop many of our guys from warming up bare chested. The only thing they were wearing on their chests was Vaseline, and I hated that for one main reason: when we broke down for position drills during pregame and I would have to throw passes to my running backs, I could *never* grip the damn footballs because they were slathered with remnants of Vaseline. The players said they put on Vaseline to block the cold. My thing was: "Just wear your damn jerseys and you'll be warm." That was their thing, and it wasn't a big deal.

Coach Simon's pregame ritual was carrying around this large sledgehammer on his shoulder like Paul Bunyan. He actually does resemble Paul Bunyan, because he is tall and husky with a long beard. Coach Simon carried that sledgehammer with him every single game.

He explained why: "In 2002, when I was a senior at Massillon, we went to a team camp at the University of Kentucky. While

Photo courtesy of J. P. Simon

J. P. Simon is NOT Paul Bunyan. Can that be proven?

we were there, the skill players competed in seven-on-sevens while the lineman competed in a big-man challenge. We competed with thirty other schools from across the country. The winning team was awarded a sledgehammer. All we talked about was how we had to bring that sledgehammer home for Coach [Steve] Studer. We used that as our battle cry throughout the events. When we won the hammer and brought it back to Coach Stu, you would have thought it was Christmas for him. He couldn't have been more proud of us. Fast-forward to 2017: I am coaching the defensive line. We go to the University of Pittsburgh for a similar team camp, where the skill players are competing in seven-on-sevens and the big men have a challenge of their own.

"I knew once I saw it that we had to win it. The first year we came in second place. I remember all off-season, all the guys talked about was wanting to go back the next year and win the hammer. Sure enough, the following year we went back, and with the final event being a tug-of-war competition for all the marbles, the Tigers pulled out the win, and we went crazy. There are still videos out there of the actual tug-of-war and the hammer ceremony. We brought the hammer back, and it became sort of a trophy for the 'trench life' guys [the linemen]. That's why we carry it around. It represents and symbolizes our workman-type mentality."

Coach Simon also told me about a "lively discussion" he had with members of the McKinley coaching staff before a Massillon-McKinley game a few years back. "The incident that happened with McKinley started when Coach Weber and Dan Reardon, who was McKinley's head coach at the time, were having a little discussion at the fifty. It seemed like they were getting a little extra friendly, so I stuck my nose in, with the hammer on my shoulder. Mind you, our hammer was a twenty-pounder, and McKinley assistant coach Chad Anderson walked over with a ten-pounder to try to be intimidating, and the jokes were flying. I asked him which local hardware store did he buy his hammer, because ours was earned, not purchased. It was pretty comical to see."

Throughout this book I have started each chapter with a section of a Coach Dave Weber letter. For this chapter and game, it needed to be more. A paragraph wouldn't do justice to his words, the history, or The Game. The letter arrived to each Massillon team member on the morning of November 2, 2019, and now it is shared with you. As you read it, before diving into the coverage of the 125th Massillon-McKinley game, I invite you to let these words sink in. I invite you to think about what the kids, on both sides of the field, must have been experiencing as all the talk, all the hype, and all the history faded away, and all that was left was The Game.

Coach Weber's "Words of Wisdom"

I live in a wonderful town. I've lived here every minute of my life. We don't have fancy stuff. We don't have a lot of newly built buildings. One of the places I love to go to is Columbus because everything is shiny and new and kind of cool. But I don't want to live in Columbus. I want to live here. What makes Massillon, Massillon, is us. It's the people. We are not fancy people. We are blue-collar. We have hard lives and not much money. What bonds this town together, and pushes us through hard times, is you. And one of the most visible indicators of that, happens tomorrow. Massillon will turn out for you.

This week has been an awesome week for you. Lots of fun stuff, hard work after school at practice, then more fun stuff at night. Yesterday was the capstone on the fun stuff. The pep rally, the parade, are things you will always remember. Season 1 has ended. McKinley Week has ended. I'm sending this after midnight because this letter is not part of McKinley Week. It is intended for the Day of Days.

You've heard it a million times this week. Beat McKinley! Maybe it feels like someone walking by you and asking "Hey, how are you doing?" Most times that is a polite phrase that no one really wants you to answer. Beat McKinley, in this town is the same as I Love You. People mean it. It is their way of signaling to each other—young, old, man, woman—that we are in this together. We are one this week and especially on this day. The weight of our little world sits on you. You will hold them up and carry them with you until the final whistle, but just at the moment you need them, they will climb down and carry you. This day of days is 30,000 residents of our town, and the alumni spread everywhere across this country having a common purpose. No one sitting in those stands for us is just there watching a game. They are playing the game with you. Every block, tackle, run, pass, interception, touchdown . . . is felt by the people in those stands. You are not alone in this tomorrow, although when you are out there, you will feel the intensity of what is unfolding, when you need it, you will feel their intensity.

McKinley Saturday is a day that stands alone. In the morning, some of you will wake up anxious. Some of you will wake up nervous. Some of you will wake up excited. Some of you will wake up joyous as the day is finally here. You will go through your morning with all the scheduled activities one final time. You will get to the stadium early before the buses for breakfast at the Eagles. When I played, it was steak and eggs in the old high school cafeteria. Then we will board the buses and go to St. Timothy's. That has always been an important part of the morning for me. Asking God for a win in a football game seemed silly. Then the former Reverend there once said, "God already knows what is in your heart. Why wouldn't you ask for it?" So, I always do. Then finally we head back to the stadium, pack up, load the buses and go. We played at Fawcett. So, I had the same experience this year's seniors are having. On the road for McKinley.

The bus ride over for me was solemn. It was solemn because I came to the realization on the 15-minute trip that it was time. The weight of the town, my family, and those who came before me and wore that uniform, was squarely on my back and on everybody sitting with me on those buses. The time had come. The Day of Days had arrived. Does telling you that on that bus trip, you assume the weight of the town and our history on your back seem like it's putting pressure on you? Damn right it's putting pressure on you. A lot of pressure. You need to understand and embrace that weight on your back. And in the 48-minute window that you've been given on Saturday, November 2, 2019, playing that game and wearing that uniform, each minute that goes by is a minute you will never get back. And how you play in that minute will build up to win or lose that game for you. You were given 48 individual minutes to play in the greatest game in high school football. It is completely on you how those minutes stack up. What happens in that window?

Do not lose this game. You don't want to live with losing this game. Because you will live with it. It will come back to haunt you one day a year, and every time you are around anything associated with Massillon Football. Because you will be in one of the classes, one of the 53, that have lost to them. You don't want to be number 54. You need to enter this game with a great fear of becoming number 54. You will never get November 2, 2019 back as a do over. You will have to live with it. And you will live with it. Don't kid yourself. So, of all the things I mentioned earlier about how you might wake up

Saturday morning, the overriding feeling you should have is one of fear, of dread. And the way you should deal with that feeling of fear is get locked in from the moment you wake up. There is no second chance. This is the Day of Days. It has been given to you.

You Do NOT Want To Lose This Game! Fear that. Deal with that. Bury that. It is your Day of Days.

Go Tigers!! Beat the living hell out of McKinley!!! That Bell goes nowhere!!!

Part 4: The War of 2019

Photo by Rocky Dorsey

An estimated crowd of over 15,000 fans packs the stands for the 125th Massillon-McKinley game on November 2, 2019.

The teams hit the field, and the balloons were released into the sky. Massillon filled its entire side of the stadium and even spilled over into part of McKinley's section. The noise was deafening. "Beat McKinley" from the north side of the stadium would generate a "Beat Massillon" from the south. But once the game started and all of the trash-talking among players subsided, it was time to get to business. McKinley was

8-1, and its only loss had been decided by one point in overtime. McKinley had a dangerous junior quarterback in Elijah Wesly, who had a run-first attitude but was getting stronger at throwing by the week. That's why this game is played in week ten. Both teams want the best version of their opponent to decimate. McKinley had a new head coach, Marcus Wattley. But he wasn't new to playing Massillon. He was the former St. Vincent-St. Mary coach. He was also the last coach to beat Massillon in a regular-season game, back in 2017. We all knew you could throw out all the records when it came to the greatest high school football rivalry in the country.

Coach Moore had been tight-lipped with the media all week about whether Aidan Longwell would start. However, we knew on Monday Aidan was good to play. He returned to practice but did not participate. By Wednesday, Aidan was at full speed, but there was no need to let the other side know which quarterback they should be preparing for.

Luckily for us, when it came to game time, Aidan was ready to go. We would have our field general for the battle of the year. But another one of our soldiers was wounded before the game even started. The night before his first McKinley game, our leading running back, Terrance Keyes, lost his grandmother. It tore him up. It was an eerie bookend to Andrew Wilson-Lamp's grandmother's passing the night before the first game. Now, as we closed out the regular season, another death weighed on one of our offensive weapons. I coached up Keyes as best as I could. I was sympathetic and tried to keep his mind on the game. Death is never easy, and having to balance that as a youth while you are playing in the biggest game of your life is something I am grateful I never had to face.

Coach Robinson, who was experiencing his first McKinley game, said, "It didn't hit me how much that game meant to people until we took the field and our side was filled to the brim with people. It was nerve-racking the whole game, because it was a war and no team could get an edge."

Coach Troxler, who was coaching in his third McKinley game, told me about his first time. "At my first Massillon-McKinley game, I was soaking up the entire day—all morning long, just enjoying it. I was not that nervous, just another big football game, right? I've coached in

Trench Life: no guts, no glory. The Massillon and McKinley lines battle it out.

some big ones, too. Then we get there and all of sudden it hit me: I'm about to coach in the biggest high school football game in the nation!!!!!! I was very nervous about calling plays in that first game. My good friend Coach Hack slaps me on the back and says, 'Trox, got some advice for you . . . don't F this up!' Thanks, Hack. Anyway, we went on to win 16-15."

As we had done the previous week, we started off slow. Which isn't that rare in a Massillon-McKinley game. It is more often than not a defensive battle, due to the fact that both teams know each other so well and have prepared for this game all year long. Both defenses were amped and ready to go. When you are in a defensive battle the key is to not turn the ball over. Late in the first quarter Massillon defensive back T. J. Williams tackled Jalen Ross for a loss on third down, forcing McKinley to punt. McKinley's punter, Xavier Black, did a sprint-out, soccer-type punt. It was a line drive, and as T. J. was running downfield the ball hit him in the helmet and McKinley recovered at the fifty. No one was upset with T. J. It was a fluke play, but a turnover nonetheless. Seven plays later Xavier Black scored on a perfectly thrown thirty-four-yard touchdown pass to the left corner of the end zone from quarterback

Elijah Wesley, with just three seconds left in the first quarter. The Tigers followed with a three-and-out, and all the noise and momentum was colored red and black for McKinley.

I'll be honest: we struggled to get things going offensively. I was waiting for Terrance to break a long run, or something. But he seemed to be bottled up and couldn't get any type of explosive run. I knew he had so much on his mind, but I was hoping he could have the kind of game legends deserve.

Terrance Keyes, Sr., commented on how the death affected his son: "You could tell it was on his mind. I really didn't know how he would play, but when the game started he was like one of those old-school cars on a cold day. You have to start it up, then you go back into the house and let it run for a minute to warm up. That was Terrance."

We finally tied the score late in the second quarter on a twelve-yard touchdown pass from Aidan Longwell to Jayden Ballard and Alex Bauer's PAT, with 2:21 left to play in the half. Jayden went up and over the McKinley defender for a breathtaking catch.

Photo by Rocky Dorsey

Jayden Ballard goes over the McKinley defender to get Massillon on the board.

McKinley went three and out and muffed the punt, which gave Massillon the ball back at the fifty with forty-eight seconds left in the half. Aidan fired a bullet to the sideline to Wilson-Lamp, who stepped out of bounds at the McKinley forty-two-yard line. With a hurry-up offense, Aidan passed to Jayden on the same side to get to the thirty-seven and a first down. On the next play, Aidan looked to pass downfield, but saw nothing. He decided to run all the way to the far side to try to get out of bounds and stop the clock. A McKinley defender, right on his tail, tackled him with a hard hit on the shoulder he had injured the previous week. Aidan clearly got the ball out-of-bounds, but the ref ruled that he was inches short of the line and signaled to keep the clock moving. Massillon had used up all of its first-half time-outs to stop the clock on McKinley's previous possession. It looked like time would run out, but Aidan wasn't getting back up. The ref blew the whistle to stop the clock for an injury time-out. Aidan writhed in pain. After what seemed like a lifetime, he was helped up and managed to stand on his own.

Zach Catrone got the call and went in for his teammate. The offensive coordinators had just as much faith in him as they did in Aidan. They called another pass play. No one was open, so Zach made a run for the sideline to stop the clock. It was a heady decision for the junior quarterback. A lesser player would have forced a throw that could have easily been intercepted, but all those games that were blowouts over the past two seasons had made Zach a hell of a backup. He got us to the thirty-five-yard line and stopped the clock, and with two seconds left in the half Alex Bauer nailed a thirty-five-yard field goal to give us our first lead of the game. I tell you, that kid was money for us all year. Alex and our punter, Magnus Haines, were special-team unsung heroes for us. We would head to the locker room with a tight lead, 10-7.

When we (Coach McConnell, Coach Leno, Coach Stone, and I) left the press box and headed to the elevator, McKinley's coaches were standing at the elevator waiting to get on. The elevator operator had held it for just the coaches, so we all had to get in together. You know how it is when you get into an elevator with a stranger? We all jammed into the elevator together—just Massillon and McKinley coaches. The door closed, and a McKinley coach said, "Pretty nice day today, huh?" We all nodded and said, "Oh yeah, it is. Great day for football, right?"

Then, *everyone* did that fake chuckle. You know that laugh like you just heard the funniest joke in the world, only it was the corniest joke in the world and you were just being polite by laughing? That was us. Then everyone put their heads down, and it was so quiet you could hear a gnat fart. Finally, the elevator got us to field level, and we got the hell off that elevator as fast as we could.

In the locker room, the players talked among themselves, used the bathroom, sought out the trainer if need be. Aidan was checked out and given the go-ahead for the second half. The coaches congregated in the office to discuss the first half and make appropriate adjustments. We then met with our units to go over the strategy for the second half. Then the press-box coaches headed back upstairs. Halftime is usually twenty minutes, which might seem long to some fans, especially when it's cold, but when you're in the locker room trying to formulate your game plan for the second half, those twenty minutes fly right by.

The second half was another defensive battle. Early on, both teams moved the ball a little, but no scores. But with only 1:28 left in the third quarter, the star running back finally broke free for a perfect forty-eight-yard run. Problem was, it was McKinley's Lameir Garrett. The Bulldogs took their second lead of the game, 14-10. There were only thirteen minutes left to play in the game, and we were down. Were we going to let McKinley spoil our undefeated regular season? Our back-to-back undefeated seasons? McKinley's fans were on their feet cheering. They hadn't beaten Massillon since 2015. They were not going to be denied. I thought of all those close games I had lost in other sports. The entire reason I wanted to coach Massillon football was to get a McKinley team. I realized I was cursed. Here I was, the running backs coach of the Massillon Tigers, and the McKinley running back had just won the game for them. I was feeling like a black cloud was following me around.

Down on the field, Terrance had something else hovering over him.

"When they went down and scored, I felt my grannie watching over me, Coach, I really did," Terrance would say to me later.

While I was panicking, our senior captain and center, Cole Jones, had a different thought. One of the things I loved about Cole (I had him in my English and senior writing classes, and he was hysterically funny, and smart) was that he was such an intelligent player and knew what was working and what wasn't. At this moment of the game, Cole stepped up. "We were on the sideline after going three and out in our series before Garrett scored," Cole said. "I looked at Terrance and said, 'Hey man, the inside zone is working. Just run right up my ass. I promise you it will be a touchdown.' He was like 'OK, I got you, bro.'" Cole said he told Coach Mazur to call inside zone runs the next time we got the ball. "We came out on first down seconds after Garrett scored, and we ran our inside zone run play that I knew would give us a touchdown," Cole said.

Terrance tore off a sixty-three-yard touchdown and gave Massillon the lead again, at 17-14. Cole continued, "The reason I knew it would work was because in our series before Garrett's touchdown, we ran a play on third down and got about eight yards. Right then and there I knew I would be able to help our right guard [junior Rager Els] pin their nose tackle inside, and that would allow Terrance to run into an open running lane. We got the play we wanted, and it worked exactly how I thought. The left side of our line had everything cut off on their side, and it was nothing but open field. I remember right before the

Seconds after McKinley scores, Terrance breaks loose for a big score.

131

THE MASSILLON TIGERS: 15 FOR 15

play, when it was called, I looked at Terrance, he looked at me, and we just nodded. We knew what was about to happen. Right after the score, I met him in the end zone, threw him up in the air, and we went back to our sideline to celebrate for a short time, because we knew we still had to go out there and win the game."

Terrance got the score, Cole had the plan, but there was an unsung hero: T. J. Williams. He showed what it meant to put ego aside and look out for your teammates. We had several mottos and slogans during the year, but one that will stand the test of time was "Team Above Self," and T. J. exemplified that.

Terrance gave the credit for that score to T. J. He told me months later, "Coach Morgan, I never told anybody this, but after [McKinley scored], T. J. ran down to me and said, 'Terrance, we need you, man. Do you need a rest? Do you need me to go back for this kickoff? You need to be fresh.' I told him, 'Yeah, good idea, go 'head, man.'"

T. J. sprinted out into kickoff receiving coverage and, in fact, received the kickoff. He had a respectable run up the middle of the field for eighteen yards to the McKinley thirty-seven, but was hit really hard and almost fumbled. *Almost.* I honestly think that if T. J. had been in a selfish state of mind, he would have fumbled. I mean, he really almost lost the ball on the hit. It was his major contribution to "TEAM" and not to "SELF." T. J.'s actions allowed Terrance to gather his thoughts and energy for his longest run of the game. That touchdown came with 1:12 left in the third quarter and gave us a 17-14 lead. The game wasn't over yet. It was still anyone's game.

The entire fourth quarter went back and forth. With 11:52 left, we had the ball in great field position at McKinley's forty-four. We drove the ball down the field and got to the fifteen. But on a third and two, Aidan threw an interception at McKinley's three, and it was returned to the eleven. That gave the Bulldogs the ball with 9:25 left in the game and a chance to put together a game-winning drive.

McKinley picked up chunks of yards, moving into our territory and eating up a lot of the clock. With just 3:07 left to play, McKinley had driven to our seventeen-yard line, facing a fourth and four at the seventeen-yard line. A field goal would tie the game; a TD would put us in a bad situation. McKinley called a timeout to think it over. I did not want them to score and lose my chance at experiencing this win. McKinley had lost the last three games against us. That meant its seniors needed this win, or the entire class would never know what it was like to beat Massillon.

McKinley's offense returned to the field. They were going for the win. It was a pass play. Quarterback Elijah Wesley was in the shotgun and faked a handoff to running back Lameir Garrett, who stayed back to pass-protect. Wesley let the ball go and had a wide-open tight end, Jasper Robinson, in the end zone. It was all over. We let a receiver get wide open. Coach Moore remembered, "We were in a situation where if McKinley scores, then all of a sudden we're now down, and they have all the momentum. We're looking at only one possession with a chance to answer that score. It would put us with our backs to the wall."

Up in the press box we had a bird's-eye view of how wide open Robinson was. Coach McConnell was pounding on the table in the press box so hard I thought he was going to break it. He was yelling, "No . . . No . . . Noo . . . Nooo . . . NOOOOOO!!!!!!" Out of nowhere, Andrew Wilson-Lamp, who hadn't played defense all year but was playing cornerback for this game, miraculously left the receiver he was guarding and ran toward the ball. He managed to find it floating in the air a split second from landing in the receiver's arms and batted the ball away. It hit the ground, and McKinley turned the ball over on

Photos courtesy of WHS-TV

Andrew Wilson-Lamp's game-saving play deconstructed:
1. AWL notices Robinson is wide open. 2. He cuts across the end zone. 3. He knocks the ball and McKinley's hope for a comeback to the ground.

downs. Our fans went crazy. I have never heard screams that loud in my life. From my vantage point in the press box, it had been clear that McKinley was going to score.

"I was guarding their outside receiver in man coverage, but I was playing off because I already knew what route he was going to run, because he was doing the same thing the entire game," Andrew explained. "So I just let him run the fade route, because he was running to the back corner of the end zone and he had no room to do anything. The other receiver, I didn't even know that he was open. I just turned, saw the ball in the air and just wanted to knock it down, at least. Then I knew I could get it because the way the ball was just floating in the air, I was like, 'Oh man, I can get this.'"

Coach Moore doesn't mince any words about the importance of Wilson-Lamp's play. He said, "It's a play that'll go down as one of the great plays in the history of the rivalry."

Just before the play, Terrance said, he was on the sideline down on one knee praying. He said he didn't want to see the play. Cole was the opposite. He said, "I wanted to see everything that was happening. I wanted to see if we were going to win or lose, and I wanted to see how it was going to play out. I just had to see it." Meanwhile, Terrance continued to torture himself. "What was going through my head was this: If I heard the crowd over there [he was pointing to McKinley's side] cheering, I knew it was over and that we lost. If I heard the crowd cheering from over here [pointing to the Massillon side], then I knew we stopped them and that we were getting the ball back. It was just too much pressure for me to watch." This WAS the McKinley game, and like Coach Weber wrote, and preached: "Hell, yeah, there was going to be pressure on these kids."

"I kept saying, 'Please, Lord, let us bring [the bell] home. Please, please pleeeeease, let us bring it home,'" Terrance said. "When I heard our crowd cheering, I knew it was time for us to put the game away."

Aidan, the consummate professional, said he didn't even realize it was fourth down. He was sitting on the bench focused on what he needed to do when the offense got back on the field. Whether we were going to be down and needing him to orchestrate a come-from-behind game-winning drive or whether he needed to pick up a few first downs to run out the clock and preserve the win, it was all the same to the three-year starter. At this point, when you added up all the long playoff runs he had been a part of, he had played in more games than the average high school player ever plays in. "I just heard our crowd erupt and I was like, 'We got the ball back. Alright, let's go. We just need a few first downs and it's over.'"

There was still enough time for McKinley to get the ball back if it forced us into a three-and-out series. There are all kinds of theories as to what to do when you have three minutes left in the game, you are seventy-three yards away from scoring, and you are holding onto a scant, three-point lead. What happened next might just be forever more known as the *Troxler Doctrine*.

"I'm thinking, 'Alright, we got the ball, we're backed up inside our thirty, and if we make a mistake down here it might cost us the game,'" Coach Troxler said. "We were all huddled over on the sideline and I looked up at Aidan and I said, 'Here we go!' We were just talking about how we're going to finish this game out, how we needed the offense to finish this thing off and not give them another opportunity at the end of the game. I never talked to Aidan about not throwing an interception— that's the WORST thing you can tell a quarterback. I just told him, 'Hey, a big mistake can be very costly right now. So be smart with the football.' He just looked at me, smiled, and said, 'I got you.' That's all that needed to be said."

This was our sequence:
• First and ten: Zion rushes for two yards
• Second and eight: Zion rushes for two yards
• Third and six: the Troxler Doctrine

Coach Troxler recounted: "I looked at [Coach Moore] and said, 'Hey, can we take a timeout?' He said, 'Yeah!' Everybody came to the sideline, and we were thinking, 'What's the best decision to do right now?' [McKinley] probably knew we were going to throw. I said, 'Alright, here we go. We're going to throw [the play] Magic.' Coach Miller was like, 'Let's do it.' I told Aidan, 'I want you to stare at Andrew. If he's open, take it. If that safety runs over the top, you just turn and throw it to Jayden. Just throw it.'"

Coach Moore has complete confidence in Troxler and his staff. He said, "I've got just an unbelievable coaching staff. A lot of them are experts at their position. When you have guys like that, the worst thing you could do is interrupt their flow. I used to do that a lot. It's counterproductive. I stay out of their way when they're calling the plays. I'm highly involved in the off-season preparation of putting our playbook together and how it's going to match our personnel, but the actual calling of the plays, I stay out of that because I have guys that are really good at what they do."

Three shots of Jayden catching Aidan's pass. The Troxler Doctrine is born.

Coach Troxler made the right call. Andrew was split wide on the right side and McKinley's safety jumped over into double coverage, which left Jayden one-on-one against a cornerback. Aidan threw one of the most perfect passes of his career, connecting with Jayden on a seventy-nine-yard touchdown pass with 1:18 left in the game, giving us a 24-14 lead and sealing the win.

"We wanted that matchup," Aidan said. "We knew by the way [McKinley] was playing that we could get it to Jayden. I swear the wind was starting to pick up a little bit, and when I let the ball go I thought I overthrew it. I said to myself, 'Oh my God, I overthrew him.' But Jayden kicked it in and got to it. It was beautiful. As I was running off the field, Coach Troxler was so excited that he broke his headset, and that was the third set he broke during the season."

Coach Troxler said, "Aidan ran off the field, we started hugging, and he started crying. It was just an unbelievable feeling."

Coach Mazur added, "I honestly think that's going to go down as one of the biggest plays in Massillon-McKinley history, because it put a dagger in McKinley and it was a great way for this group of seniors to end the regular season."

Coach Miller said, "You know, thankfully it worked out. I mean, Aidan dropped back, and it was one of the most beautiful balls I have ever seen. And just all the emotion of that game . . . I don't really know how to describe it. With a full house there at Tom Benson Hall of Fame Stadium, with a tight game in the fourth quarter, I could barely hear anybody on the sidelines because the fans were going nuts. And for us to make that play to seal that win was one of the greatest memories that I've ever had as a coach."

The team gathered by the away stands and formed a circle. Players and coaches hugged one another, jumped around, and had tears in their eyes. Coach Moore gave quick soundbites to the radio and TV reporters on the field. Players sat on the bell and rang it as others awaited their turn. But even in the midst of the greatest celebration of the year, J. P.

Ethan Tobin rides the victory bell following a 24-14 win over McKinley.

blew the whistle and the team formed a circle to drop and do fifteen push-ups. Over the McKinley speaker, the home announcer Scott Davis said he wasn't aware there would be after-game calisthenics. The Massillon faithful called out those fifteen push-ups with pride. Even after a close game like this one, we had our routine to remind us there was more work to do.

Sophomore quarterback Tanner Pierce, who was our offensive scout team player of the year, described the experience: "After beating McKinley, it was the best feeling in the world. Right after the game running towards the bell, doing the alma mater right in front of the student section, having the times of our lives in the locker room with my teammates, it was just an amazing feeling."

Coach Robinson remembered, "When we won, the relief set in inside the locker room when [Superintendent Paul 'Sal' Salvino] told the team how much beating McKinley meant to the whole town. We took a picture as a coaching staff in front of the bell, and I can remember that like yesterday."

It also was a great regular-season ending for Terrance, who was named the most valuable player of the game. "I just started bursting out crying, especially after looking for my dad and seeing him in the crowd," he said. "I could see he was crying too. When we got in the locker room, I remember thanking everybody for making me feel like part of their family." Terrance was standing in the middle of the locker room while everyone was down on one knee, and he kept saying, "y'all . . . y'all . . . y'all . . ." like he wasn't part of the Massillon family. That's when Coach Weber stepped in and said, "Terrance, wait. No more of that 'y'all.' It's WE!! . . . US!! You are part of this family, and you have been since the first day you got here." Terrance got emotional recounting this moment to me. "I had never experienced anything like that," he said through tears, months after the game. "It just felt like, 'Man, I finally did my part for the team.' I wasn't a newcomer anymore. I felt the love from my guys. We had a lock-in with the team at the beginning of the preseason, and I remember Coach Weber being passionate and yelling and screaming about us earning the right to be a true Tiger, and there I was on the inside feeling like an outsider. So for him to step in after the McKinley game like he did, those words coming out of his mouth about me being part of the family was insane. It was a great moment for me. I love him for saying that about me."

In every Massillon-McKinley game a hero is born. Was it Jayden's reception? Was it Andrew Wilson-Lamp knocking down the pass with his finger tips? Was it Terrance's explosive touchdown run? Was it Cole Jones and the rest of the offensive line? Alex Bauer's kick? Aidan's time management? History will decide what is remembered from this game. For me, it was the team that I was a part of. Terrance felt part of the family. I did too. I came into this with no wins against McKinley. I rang that victory bell and felt every bit of what it meant to be a Massillon Tiger. Kickoff for this game had been 2:00 p.m. It was after five by the time we were leaving the stadium. It felt like it should be midnight. But the night wasn't over yet. In Tiger Town, there is always one more tradition.

Photo courtesy of Erik Longwell

Aidan holds the Rivalry Trophy while the players celebrate in the locker room following the 129th meeting of the rivals.

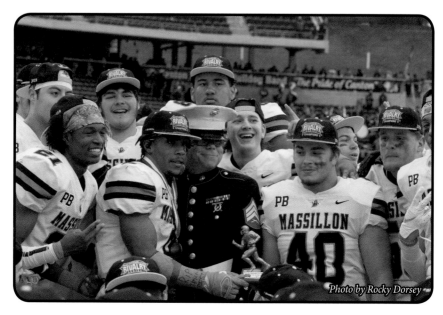

Terrance Keyes is awarded the most valuable player of the game from a representative of the US Marines while his teammates gathers around.

The Tigers serenade their fans before dropping to give 15.

Brain Trust: the coaches who devised the winning game plan.

The victory bell is on display at the high school for another year.

TIME OUT!

One of the great things about coaching and teaching at Massillon is that I had the opportunity to interact with my players on the field, but more importantly inside the classroom. It was a great reward watching our players have success where it's most important in their lives. Junior defensive tackle C. J. Harris was one of my students in English 10 during the school year. He was a quiet kid, but a hard worker. On the football field, there was nothing quiet about him. He played like a beast.

C. J. broke his right hand (he's right-handed) in the McKinley game fighting off a block and never knew it was broken. "I didn't hear anything pop or anything like that; it just felt like a bruise," he said. "I played the rest of the game, and after the game my adrenalin was pumping because we just beat McKinley, so I didn't feel anything." C. J. said his hand started to swell on Sunday, and by Monday's practice he knew it was time to see our training staff.

"They told me to go get it X-rayed right away. I went to the hospital right then, and when I left the hospital, I had a cast."

C. J. played the rest of the season with that cast on, and he said it was tough to make tackles. He said his strategy was to try to tackle a runner by the arm or around the neck. "That was easier than trying to wrap around the waist."

Coach Leno said C. J. was a key part of his defense.

"We are looking for C. J. to be a huge contributor next year. He's the kind of kid you know will play hard for you."

Part 5: Post Game

After we enjoyed all the hugs and picture taking inside the locker room, and once we boarded the buses, everyone was literally bouncing off the seats. Everything we had worked so hard for since winter conditioning became a reality. It will always be about beating McKinley. We got on the road for the short drive back to Massillon. We were driving along Route 30 and came up to the Richville Drive exit, which takes us back to school, but barreled right past it. I tapped Coach Weber, whom I always sat behind on our bus, on the shoulder and asked, "Where are we going?" He said, "Oh, you don't know! Wait until you see this. You're going to shit your pants." Where could we possibly go that would be more exciting than what we had just experienced?

We exited at Route 21 North exit and stayed on that for about a minute, until we came to Walnut Street near downtown. We made a few turns to get to Lincoln Way, the main street running through town, and into downtown Massillon. It was the same road that last night's parade had traveled. When we made the turn, I thought I saw someone in the middle of the street. I was wrong. It wasn't someone. It was everyone. I couldn't believe my eyes. I let my window down in the old yellow school bus, stuck my head out, and all I saw was a sea of orange and black in the street and on the sidewalks. Traffic couldn't move. Horns blasted every few seconds. The cheering was deafening. It looked—and sounded— like a miniversion of the 2016 Cleveland Cavaliers NBA championship parade in downtown Cleveland, which I also experienced. This town just never ceases to amaze me. We hadn't won the state championship; it was just the end of the regular season.

All four buses stopped in front of the Lincoln Theater. We all got out, and people surrounded the doors. The players found their families or friends. Everyone was hugging and high-fiving. People danced. They cheered and cried. We walked around for about twenty minutes, soaking it all in. Then we all got back on the bus and headed back to school. After all, we had a game plan to get to. In six days we would be playing our first playoff game. I still have no idea how the kids were able to come down from something like this in twenty-four hours.

Coach Weber, who had been through this scene more times than any

Photo by David Lee Morgan, Jr.

Thousands gather in downtown Massillon to greet the team and celebrate the win.

of us, described it perfectly: "I first experienced going through downtown after my senior McKinley game. I can remember after beating them, leaning out of the window, slapping the hands of people I knew and didn't know. The joy in their eyes, and the feeling of that joy being given back to me. Years later, my daughter got to experience it as a cheerleader on a trip back into town after a win over there. My son got to experience it his sophomore year. A picture, which ended up in the coffee-table book produced by Kent State University, captured that moment for him forever. It is the kind of thing you only experience here, in a community that dearly loves their Tigers and lives especially for that day and that game. Riding through town on the bus after winning that game is the closest thing in your life where you will ever feel like being one of the gods."

Coach Troxler said, "Even though you are drained from the emotional roller coaster the game is, it's always exciting to go downtown. Seeing everyone in orange and black, it makes you just so happy. I've never seen an entire city just generally happy like I did that day. The entire city is there, partying in the streets and celebrating a huge Tiger win! We stopped the buses because we could not get through on Lincoln Way. We just got out of the van to greet the great fans. I just could not believe it. Just how happy everyone was. That day really showed me how much Massillon football and that game means to the city of Massillon. It is a day I will never forget. It's a day I look forward to like Christmas!"

Sophomore offensive and defensive lineman Nick Hatheway, who was our scout team defensive player of the year, said: "The energy that came from everyone in the bus was pure happiness and relief. We fulfilled the standards of one of the oldest traditions anywhere in high school football. I vividly remember coming off the bus to a massive crowd of orange and black. I remember looking for my mom to give her the biggest hug and kiss. I started to realize in that moment that after being a scout team player throughout the year and getting beat up every week, it was worth every ounce of pain I endured just to feel what it's like to be a Massillon Tiger."

"Let me just say the aftermath felt like I had just played a triple-overtime game in college," said Coach Robinson, who was an offensive lineman at Bowling Green State University. This was Chip's first year coaching, but unlike me, it wasn't his last year. "Everyone wanted me to stay out all night, including my wife, but I just wanted to eat and go home to sleep! After we won, it was awesome, because you felt like you won the AFC Championship, but still had the Super Bowl in a few weeks. When we pulled in downtown, there were no less than 10,000 people. I was given hugs by so many people I still don't know. It was awesome. People were crying. People were smoking victory cigars. The whole town partied from 6:00 p.m. to 3:00 a.m. It was nuts. Every bar and restaurant was packed. The line to get to Taco Bell spilled out onto Lincoln Way. The day was memorable from start to finish, but holy smokes, it was exhausting."

Sophomore Tanner Pierce said, "I remember getting on the bus and heading downtown with all the other sophomores, with Coach Weber and Coach Morgan. I remember talking about how bad we wanted to beat them again for the next two years so we can keep the bell and have our class go 4-0 against McKinley. Once we got downtown, I remember seeing the whole city of Massillon down there celebrating with us. Everyone was getting pictures with all the players and having a great time. I can't wait to be back at Tom Benson stadium my senior year and come back to Massillon with the bell, celebrating downtown with our amazing city and enjoying another win over Canton McKinley."

Coach Weber put a bow on it: "When I walked through downtown last year, I still relished it, but I tried to make sure whomever I was with on the bus experienced it, because a win in that game is never guaranteed, and each opportunity to be able to do that might be your last." -

THE SCORE BOARD

Teams	Q1	Q2	Q3	Q4	F
Massillon Tigers (10-0)	0	10	7	7	24
Canton McKinley (8-2)	7	0	7	0	14

POST SEASON

Sketch by Dan Studer

Chapter 17
Warren Harding

Our first test on the road to the state championship was a rematch against my alma mater, Warren Harding. I was excited about this game, but not as excited as I was for the week-three game at Warren, when I was going back home. Massillon had finished No. 1 not only in the state AP poll, but also in the computer points that determined whom we would meet in the playoffs. It meant we would get to have one last home game. Warren finished its season 7-3 and was the number-eight seed.

We made it to the postseason, the playoffs. It was about being focused, taking care of the opponent in front of us, because at this point it was one-and-done—lose and go home. The 15 for 15 could turn into 11 for 15 in the blink of an eye. There goes the dream of playing for a state championship. It was more about coming out and making sure we took care of what we needed to, not overlooking anyone, and being mentally and physically prepared to play. After the emotional high of McKinley Week and the big win, we had to make sure the kids didn't think it was all smooth sailing from here

With all the talk about the week-eleven trap, the kids were focused all week. We had played Warren before and manhandled them. We were expecting to win, but also committed to doing our jobs. There was no disappointment for me when it came to the kids. It wasn't until just before kickoff that I felt my first disappointment. I looked over at the visiting stands and saw a sparse, and I mean sparse, turnout from Warren supporters.

I understood it was a cold evening, probably the coldest of the season. Game-time temperature was thirty degrees. And I also understood that maybe deep in their minds the Warren players, and maybe even the fans, knew this was a game they couldn't win, or at best a long shot. Still, the small crowd shocked me, and I felt some sadness. I looked at the Massillon side, and every seat was filled. This was such a shame. Back in the seventies, eighties, nineties, and 2000s, those visiting stands would've been packed. I understand things have changed over the years. Maybe the following in Warren isn't the same. And maybe in the years that I've been in Massillon I've become spoiled as to how amazing the community support is for high school football. I'm not knocking Warren Harding, the players, or even the coaching staff. Head Coach Steve Arnold is a great friend of mine.

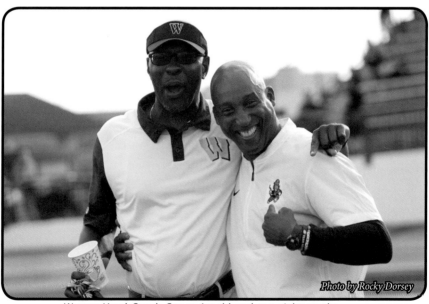

Photo by Rocky Dorsey

Warren Head Coach Steve Arnold and me eight weeks
before the rematch

148

What surprised me about the game itself was how the Warren Harding players lost any type of competitiveness. In the second half there was no fight at all. We led 27-0 at halftime, and then scored twenty-eight points in the third quarter. It was a mauling. Final score: 55-0. I don't care how good Massillon was. You shouldn't score twenty-eight points in the third quarter of a playoff game. I will be honest: it wasn't that we were that good. My Warren Harding team just wasn't trying. I could see it in Harding's eyes and body language coming out of halftime: the Raiders didn't even want to finish the game. I could see that in the effort, or the lack thereof. In fact, after one touchdown late in the third quarter, one of our TV play-by-play announcers pointed out that Warren Harding players were just standing there during the extra-point attempt. They did not even try to rush or block it. They looked like they didn't want to be there. I hate to say this about my alma mater and those players and that coaching staff, but that's exactly what it looked like. I say it because it burned me up inside. I am a Tiger, of course. But I still care and support my hometown team. I want them to be great. I want them to be competitive.

At about 7:30 the following morning, I received a text from Steve Arnold. It read: "Boona, how many of your coaches coach another sport

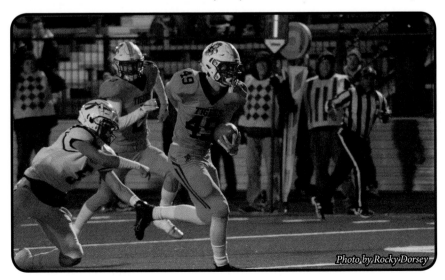

Photo by Rocky Dorsey

Caiden Woullard scores on a fumble recovery, boosting our lead to 41-0 late in the third quarter.

besides football?" (Boona was the nickname my mom gave me at birth, and to this day everyone from Warren and my Youngstown State friends call me that.) I knew why Steve sent me that text, and I called him back. Based on what had happened the night before, I figured he was trying to figure out the level of commitment within his own coaching staff, because of the way his kids had played against us. I answered his question this way: "Steve, we have one or two who coach track, and they do that because we have a lot of football players who run track. But the rest of the staff coach football all year long, man. They live, breathe, embody Massillon football. It's all about the obligation to tradition they feel they have to uphold. And that's why they came here in the first place."

Steve responded, "That's what I thought. So tell me this, Boona: why is Massillon so different? What do they do differently?"

"Steve, we have this slogan on T-shirts and sweatshirts that reads 'EDMF.' There's one interpretation of it that the coaching staff understands, but the main interpretation is 'Every Day Massillon Football.' It's a culture of pride and community and nonstop support that has never changed for decades, Steve. Warren has changed. You don't have that anymore there, and sadly you will never have that. You know I hate to say that, because I love my hometown."

"I know you do. Well, I'm going to fix some things, and we'll be back."

I said, "I know you will."

Meanwhile, the Saturday after the Warren game, a good friend of mine, David "Worm" Baugh, who is one of the most knowledgeable high school football fans in the state, and a die-hard supporter of every Warren Harding team, wrote this post on his Facebook page:

"I haven't missed a Warren G. Harding football game (home or away) in 22 years. I've witnessed the ins and outs of what it takes for football programs (not just Harding) to be great. Without getting into specifics, Warren asked for last night's result and it had nothing to do with the kids who played their hearts out on the field. Many people complain about 'numbers' and declining enrollment, but Massillon is in the exact same boat we're in. We're literally identical, but the difference is that they invest in and empower their youth to do great things. They could compete with anybody in Ohio this year and I'll personally argue that their last two teams (2018 and 2019) are the best from their modern era. Massillon is every bit as good now as they were in the early 2000's. The Massillon Tigers aren't '55 points better' than the Warren G. Harding Raiders. Their community is simply '55 points better' than ours. And the bad part is that it could've been much worse."

I am hoping my hometown and alma mater will turn this around. Massillon and Warren have battled for too many years to let that competitive spirit fade away.

One playoff game was done. As the night went on, we knew what lurked ahead. Last year we had made it to the state championship and faced the Akron Hoban dynasty. Hoban had won the last four state championships. This year they were in our region. That meant that in two weeks, if everything played out as expected, we were going to have a rematch of last year's state championship in the third week of the playoffs. Our team wanted revenge, the town wanted revenge, and the entire state was looking forward to it as well. But we had another team standing in our way before we got our rematch. We found out that night that next week, our opponent would be the Perry Panthers. Perry and Massillon had quite a sordid history. Revenge would have to wait while we faced the closest high school in geographical distance to Massillon. There was no love lost between these backyard foes. This was gonna get ugly, and fast.

THE SCORE BOARD

Teams	Q1	Q2	Q3	Q4	F
Massillon Tigers (11-0)	13	14	28	0	55
Warren Harding (7-4)	0	0	0	0	0

Chapter 18
Massillon Perry

Stark County football is a maze of history, passion, pride, and possibly more than just a dash of anger. In the beginning, there were the two beasts of football in Stark County: Massillon and McKinley. As industry grew in the area, suburbs started to pop up, and several local high schools started to splinter off from those two giants. Massillon Perry High School was one of them. The school is located just a few miles from Washington High School. Coach Dave Weber, our Tiger historian, put it this way: "They worked in the same factories that once employed tens of thousands, just as Massillon people did. Once Perry High School opened its doors, the people in Perry started to change. Rightly so, they developed pride in their school. But most of them forgot where they came from. They came from the same school that I come from. They were the same people."

A rivalry game is determined by the game, not the community. Facts are facts. Over the years, Massillon had compiled a 15-2 record against Perry. Not exactly the stuff that rivalries are made of. Perry hasn't beat Massillon in this century. A similar thing can be said about Massillon and Cleveland Saint Ignatius High School, a private Division I school in Cleveland. Massillon is 1-12 against Saint Ignatius. It might be a rivalry game to us, but it is unlikely to be as meaningful for Ignatius. That doesn't mean Perry isn't a big game. The geographic proximity and family ties between the two communities add a lot of spice to the game. I asked sports reporter Chris Easterling, who has covered both schools for over twenty years for *The Independent*, to sum up just what it is about Massillon-Perry that makes it stand apart from other games.

Massillon/Perry
by Chris Easterling

Massillon versus Perry is a rivalry that on the surface is hard to find. The two schools, located less than five miles apart, had played only seventeen times going into the 2019 playoffs, and even those meetings were far from consistent. The longest sustained run of games between the two came between 1978 and 1985. Other than that, there were three games in two seasons, 1999 and 2000, one of which was a playoff meeting; they also played in a 2006 playoff game, as well as a regular-season series from 2012-15.

Maybe the best way to describe the sentiment between the two is big brother/little brother, with a little bit of jilted-ex syndrome. Massillon, obviously, has been the football behemoth for generations. Perry, though, has grown into one of the most consistent programs in the area, particularly during head coach Keith Wakefield's two stints spanning thirty-plus years at the school. The Panthers went to back-to-back Division II state championship games in 2015 and 2016. Still, Perry's always trying to get recognition on its own, away from its more famous neighbor.

Perry's produced plenty of good football players in that time as well. Really good players, in fact. The added bitterness that exists between the two is in large part because a number of those good Perry players over the years ultimately end up, one way or the other, at Massillon. That came to a head in 1999 when Wakefield—who had coached at Massillon in the early 1970s under Bob Commings—

and Perry filed an official recruiting complaint with the Ohio High School Athletic Association against Massillon over running back Jesse Scott. Perry alleged Scott was recruited to play for the Tigers in his senior season, an allegation that the OHSAA upheld. However, most of the punishment—including a playoff ban—was subsequently overturned on appeals by Massillon.

It is that fact, more than anything else, that has led to the sparsity of meetings between the neighbors. Wakefield acknowledged that his feelings about Massillon are complicated. "People think I hate them," he told *The Independent* in the lead-up to the playoff meeting. "I don't really feel that way about the community. I feel that way about the recruiting. I don't worry about it. My experience there was pretty good with Bob. He was special."

∗∗∗

The mayor of Massillon is Kathy Catazaro-Perry, a Perry product. "I'm an outsider," she said. "I didn't grow up in Massillon. I grew up in Perry. I coached cheerleading for Perry, I was the PTA president. I was ingrained in Perry. When I married my husband, we moved to Massillon, and I ran for office. I never did think I would win, but the people in Massillon welcomed me in. I won and became a council member."

The excitement for the game was off the charts. At least it was off the seatings charts, that's for sure. The state of Ohio had unveiled a new ticket system for the playoffs in 2019. Tickets for all the games were being sold online at the OHSAA website. In the past you had to be a season ticket holder in Massillon to get first crack at a playoff ticket. Now all you needed was an Internet connection. The OHSAA decides where the games are played and when tickets go on sale, and also keeps all the money minus $1 per ticket, which goes to the school that sold the ticket. Massillon and Perry are about three miles apart. The game was placed in Greene County at Lake High School, about forty-five minutes away each team. So teams that were located six minutes apart would be driving eight times that distance to play each other, as would fans from the two communities. Blue Streak Stadium has an Astroturf field and is a magnificent facility for Lake, but it wasn't quite big enough to handle a game of this size. It's capacity is listed at 6,000. (That includes standing room.) Tickets went on sale at 10:00 a.m. on November 16. By 10:04 people were reporting on message boards that they couldn't get tickets. By 10:08 it was officially listed as sold-out.

Parents were livid. Some of these players would be suiting up for the final time, at least in their high school uniforms, and parents couldn't get tickets. What no one knew at 10:09 was that more tickets were on the way.

Timothy Todorani is a longtime Tiger fan and the manager of Howard's Tiger Rags, a downtown Massillon store specializing in team gear. He was shut out from buying tickets that morning. He said, "I tried getting on the website, but it kept kicking me off, and it wouldn't let me purchase tickets. I wasn't getting in. Within a few minutes, they were sold out."

Beau Rugg, assistant commissioner of the OHSAA, said, "We put a limited amount of tickets online. I think we had three thousand up. It was crazy." The fact that three thousand tickets were sold in under eight minutes lets you know how much demand there was for this game. Fans had hoped that the game would be played at the McKinley/Pro Football Hall of Fame stadium. But that field is owned by the NFL. Rugg said, "I called Akron University's InfoCision Stadium; they had a game that week. I called the Hall of Fame stadium, and they couldn't do it. They had a different situation. I had picked four stadiums that I felt could host the game. I reached out to both schools' [athletic directors] and said, 'This is what we have. You guys tell me which stadium you want to use.' They both agreed that Lake was the best way to go. I don't usually give the schools the option, but in this case I did, because I knew it was gonna be crazy. They needed to know what they were in for."

Message boards, Twitter, and Facebook were all aflame with anger and the fear that there would not be enough seats for fans who wanted to see the two schools compete. The main problem was that no one had been told that tickets had been held back for each school.

Rugg continued, "We only put a limited amount of tickets online. We gave each school fifteen hundred tickets for them to take care of the players' families. I took a lot of grief from people for the decision. People want to decide at the last minute to go, an hour before game time, because they are used to that. But if you go to any big sporting or music events, things sell out. There was a lot of energy around this. But we did hold some tickets back and gave them to the school. We would never cut them out."

Fans lined up in the arctic weather for over two hours before the gates opened to vie for the bleacher seats. The rest of the ticket holders would be forced to stand around the fence that looked down at the field. Lake did a great job hosting the event. They had food trucks with tons of hot chocolate ready for the game. This game could have been played two hours away and fans from Perry and Massillon still would have driven to see it.

Timothy Todorani ended up getting a ticket from a generous customer. He said, "During the week, tickets kept popping up. Someone was in the store, and when they heard I didn't get a ticket, they gave me two. It ended up being OK. There was a lot of fear the stadium wouldn't be able to accommodate. I ended up standing up against the fence. The stands were probably about four-fifths full. There were a couple of pockets open, but most people were standing around."

Afterward, it was said there was enough room, because the extra seats released to the schools didn't sell out. However, the game was also broadcast live on television in Stark County, and many casual fans, after being initially shut out or hearing how difficult it was to get a ticket, wound up staying home and watching the game from the comfort of their warm living room. In truth, interest in the game was greater than the stadium could accommodate.

One of the things I'll never forget was the bus ride to Lake High School. Our resource officer at the time, Caleb Ogletree, was one of the coolest cops on the planet. He was young, everyone respected him, and he got along with all the students, even if he had to put them in line a time or two. I was really impressed with Ogletree's driving skills. The way he escorted our buses from Massillon to Lake High School looked like something out of the *Fast & Furious* movies. Officer Ogletree would drive up to an intersection, turn on his cruiser lights, and hit the horn as our buses drove through the traffic lights. He would then speed up and ride on the berm of the road, passing all of the buses to get in front, and would do it again at the next intersection. It was quite impressive.

This was a game that had so much drama surrounding it, because so many of our coaches and players had experiences with Perry that weren't, let's say, amicable. A lot of our players, including Aidan Longwell, Cole Jones, Caiden Woullard, Andrew Wilson-Lamp, Preston and Jerron Hodges, and Isaiah Roberson, grew up in Perry. They played football in the Perry Youth leagues, but decided to move to Massillon or go to Massillon because of its football program. Being an outsider to all this, I saw it and understood it. Perry fans never liked that those kids left. They considered those kids and their families traitors. At the same time, Massillon's program has long been accused of recruiting players from other schools, districts, even states. Back in the day, Massillon was known to hold players back a year in eighth grade so that they were at an advantage once they started their freshman year in high school. That wasn't a rumor. It was a fact. In the movie *Go Tigers!* some Massillon players admit as much, saying they were held back just to gain an advantage on the football field, under the guise that they needed the year to mature "mentally."

So there was a lot of animosity between the two communities, which butted up against each other geographically. Similar animosity existed between longtime Perry Head Coach Keith Wakefield and some of the Massillon coaches.

"The game itself wasn't really like this big rivalry or revenge type of game for me," Andrew Wilson-Lamp said. "I mean, it was a playoff game, and we needed to focus on winning so we could move on. I didn't start taking it personally until I went on Snapchat one day and saw that they had all the peoples' names who left Perry to go to Massillon on tombstones. That was it for me."

Erik Longwell, Aidan's father, laughed off the idea that Massillon recruited Aidan. "He was never recruited. We were never guaranteed anything. We were guaranteed a chance to be a part of the best high school football tradition." In fact, he went on to say, when Aidan came to the school he was overlooked during his first team banquet.

Erik Longwell said, "Aidan played a little bit of varsity football as a freshman. When we went to the banquet, you know how they have those place mats where they have all the players' names on it? Aidan's name was left off it. I didn't cry. I didn't moan. I didn't say much other

Photo by Rocky Dorsey

Nancy, Aidan, and Erik Longwell on senior night.

than to the former offensive coordinator Coach Cooper. He found out and wasn't very happy about it. That one moment was a motivating factor for Aidan to work harder. After the banquet, I went up to Coach Moore in a respectful manner and said, 'Coach Moore, Aidan is going to do great things here at Massillon High School. Nobody's going to ever forget his name, again.' I shook his hand and walked out." [Laughs]

There was a lot of trash talk and bravado being displayed on both sides. But when the game started, we took care of business. We scored on all five possessions in the first half. We opened the game with a fifteen-play, seventy-eight-yard scoring drive, then scored touchdowns on the next four drives. Perry scored late in the second quarter. We took a 35-7 lead into halftime, which ended up being the final score.

Aidan put up phenomenal numbers; he was nineteen of twenty-six for 337 yards and five touchdowns with no interceptions. Jayden Ballard had ten catches for 185 yards and two touchdowns, and Andrew Wilson-Lamp had eight catches for 142 yards and three touchdowns. The defense was led by senior cornerback Luke Murphy, a Kent State recruit, who had thirteen tackles.

With all the buildup during the week, we just came out and took care of business. There really wasn't much happening at the game. The drama came after the game. I was in the locker room and heard a

Photo courtesy of the Erik Longwell Collection

Aidan connects with Andrew Wilson-Lamp for a TD in the Perry game.

screaming match outside the door. Coach Moore told me to go outside and see what was going on. I stepped outside the locker room and saw Aidan's dad, Erik Longwell, and a few Massillon fans in a shouting match with Perry fans to the point where police officers had to come and move the crowds along so that things didn't get out of hand. That's how intense the atmosphere was after the game. Had it gone on longer, I'm sure there would've been a brawl. Erik Longwell said, "It was a lot about bullying and the tombstones they had hanging in the school." Before the game or after the game, it was evident how much these two communities absolutely despise one another.

We didn't have time to linger on Perry. Everyone was interested in the other regional playoff game, Hoban against Mayfield. We all wondered if we would be facing Hoban again next week. When we got on the bus, we heard that Hoban was trailing 17-14 with 1:22 left in the game. If Hoban lost, our path to the state game would seem a lot easier. But then we couldn't get revenge for last year. Would a state title feel as earned if we didn't knock off Hoban? Everyone on the bus was refreshing Twitter feeds and texting friends to get the play-by-play for the last minute. Hoban had the ball at the thirteen-yard line, with no time-outs. It was fourth down, with 1:10 left in the game. The Knights could have kicked a field goal and tied the score, but instead they went for it. Scrambling out of the pocket, quarterback Shane Hamm threw a thirteen-yard touchdown pass, giving Hoban a 21-17 win. The rematch was at hand. Hoban 2.0 was about to happen..

As we drove back in the dark, I was tired. The traffic was crazy. Everyone from Massillon and Perry was driving on the same roads back to the same part of town. After the backyard brawl against our "little brother," we now had the regional championship game coming up. Massillon had won it the last two years in its division; Hoban had won it the last five in its division. This year, both teams were in the same division. Only one would win and move on. I looked out the window, and it was like I could see Hoban sitting at the top of the next hill. I was anxious to find out what would happen next. I sure didn't expect that six days later, one of our star players would be taken out of school in handcuffs and carted off to jail on a felony charge.

THE SCORE BOARD

Teams	Q1	Q2	Q3	Q4	F
Massillon Tigers (12-0)	14	21	0	0	35
Massillon Perry (9-3)	0	7	0	0	7

Chapter 19
Akron Hoban
(Regional Championship)

I was so proud of the way we handled business against Perry and didn't get caught up looking past the Panthers for a rematch against Hoban. After the Perry win, we had earned facing Hoban once again. The Tigers had lost only one game in 2018 and 2019. That loss was to the Hoban Knights in the 2018 state championship game, 42-28. In that game we were down 34-7 in the second half but rallied back with twenty-one unanswered points to pull within 34-28 with 9:13 left in the game. We had Hoban facing a fourth-and-two situation, and we had all the momentum in the stadium, which felt like the entire world. Hoban called a time-out, and when the players came back onto the field they were lined up in punt formation. In a bold move, they faked the punt and got the first down. They not only got the yards they needed, but also stole the momentum away from us. They scored on that drive, putting the game away and capping the team's fourth-consecutive state championship.

We had a great week of practice. Massillon had won the regional championship many times, so there wasn't really any reason for us to treat this week differently. It was week thirteen, nothing more. True, this week we were facing the current Division II dynasty team, ranked in the top twenty in the country across all divisions, but we felt we had one of the best Massillon teams in history, if not the best. The record books backed up that claim. The kids practiced hard. The coaches set up a great game plan. We were ready to go.

But then the unexpected happened. It was Thursday, November 21. The Akron police came to Massillon High School just twenty-four hours before our game with Akron's top football program. They put Terrance Keyes, Jr., in handcuffs and took him off to jail. Our star running back, who had amassed 1,504 yards up to that point, was arrested by the city that housed the school we were playing the next day. Was he arrested for something he allegedly did that day? The night before? Earlier in the week? No, he was arrested for an incident that allegedly took place over four months prior. It seemed odd, because Terrance had played the entire season up to this point without one mention of this charge or any actions being taken against him. Then he gets arrested the day before the regional championship game. That must have been one heck of a coincidence that they got a break in the case twenty-four hours before game time.

As of the printing of this book, a portion of the case is still pending. It obviously involves a student of mine who means a great deal to me. So I want to be respectful. I can't say that all journalists, tweeters, and bloggers had the same standards when it came to reporting on this story. Radio shows and the Internet went with all kinds of speculation on the day of the game. The reason his name got out at all was because the Akron police somehow put Terrance's older brother's birthday— and not Terrance's—on the arrest sheet, which made him an adult, not a juvenile. Another unfortunate coincidence, I guess.

The media hyped it up all day long. Should Terrance be allowed to play if he had been arrested? Would Massillon have to forfeit the game if Terrance walked on the field?

Terrance was arrested on a felony assault charge, but no one knew the specifics or what was going to happen. Most of the Tiger team found out at practice on Thursday. We were worried for our family member; we were concerned for our brother. Terrance was kept in jail overnight, appeared in front of a judge Friday morning, and was released. The police report from the Akron Municipal Court read that the case was DWOP, which meant Dismissed Without Prejudice, on Thursday, November 21, 2019, at 3:03 p.m. Why, if the case was dismissed on Thursday afternoon, was Terrance held until Friday morning? Another mystery.

On Friday, the day of the game, Terrance came to my room around lunchtime. He looked dejected, tired, hurt, and confused. He looked like he had dealt with a lot of stress. The room was empty except for Terrance and me. He didn't say much about what was going on. He told me that it wasn't like it sounded. I didn't judge him, because I believed in him. I just told him I was glad he was back, and safe. The night before McKinley, his grandmother had passed away; the night before Hoban he was locked up in a jail cell. This was my student, my running back, and a kid I truly cared about. It was heartbreaking for me. I felt powerless to protect him. All I could do was let him know I was there.

As for the game, the atmosphere was electric at the University of Akron's InfoCision Stadium. Since the game was held at a university stadium, tickets were not an issue. Massillon filled its side of the stadium. It felt like everyone in town made the thirty-five-minute drive to Akron. The big stadium, the cold weather, the fans—it felt like a state championship game, even though we knew NOT to make it seem like that. To us, it was just another important playoff game on our way to reaching week fifteen. It just so happened that Hoban was in our way. Hoban was on a streak of five regional championships, four state championships, and twenty-one playoff wins. That was all. Massillon has long struggled to beat parochial schools, which were free to get their players from anywhere. We titled the game #TraditionVsTuition.

We took a 7-0 lead with 6:30 left in the first quarter thanks to our very own "Triple-A": a fifty-three-yard touchdown pass from (Aidan) Longwell to (Andrew) Wilson-Lamp and the extra point by (Alex) Bauer. We scored on a four-play drive that took just 2:21 off the clock. Do you think Hoban was fazed? Hell, no! A team trying to win its fifth-consecutive state championship doesn't get rattled just because a team scores a touchdown on them in the first quarter. The Knights came right back and tied the score on a forty-yard touchdown pass from

Photo courtesy of @spencito_ on Twitter

Massillon had lost just one game over the past two seasons: to Hoban.
Who would win the rematch?

quarterback Shane Hamm to Brayden Fox and an extra point by Charlie Durkin. Hoban, not to be outdone by our quick score, did it in two plays and twenty-six seconds.

We weren't fazed by Hoban's quick score either, and we took a 14-7 lead when Zion Phifer scored on a nine-yard pass from Aidan with 1:02 left in the opening quarter. In the second quarter, Hoban put together an impressive twelve-play, seventy-eight-yard drive and tied the game with 6:30 left before halftime, scoring on a four-yard touchdown run by Victor Dawson and the extra point by Durkin. Massillon got the ball back with a few minutes to go in the half and managed to reach Hoban's thirty-one-yard line. With only seven seconds left in the half, Alex Bauer nailed a field goal, putting us up 17-14.

The second half was a defensive battle. Both teams' units were incredible. They were perfect, if there is such a thing in football. It was a battle royal for our defense, after weeks of watching our offense provide the fireworks. Terrance and Zion were trying to get something going, but couldn't manage a first down in the entire third quarter. We were playing it safe, since we clung to a three-point lead, so it was a game of punting and field position. Every punt felt like a forfeiture of the momentum we would need to take out Goliath, and every defensive stop felt like we had grabbed it back.

Coach Moore recalled Terrance taking a rough hit: "Terrance got hit in the ribs in the middle of the game. He took a really good shot, and that was the first time I realized that he wasn't wearing a rib protector. That hampered him in the second half of the game. Then we have Zion step up like he had all year."

With 6:28 left in the fourth quarter, the Knights got the ball back on their own thirty-four-yard line. They had plenty of time to put together a comeback drive, and they started to move the ball. Hamm started driving Hoban down field, and all of a sudden things weren't looking good for us. There was one play where it looked as if we had Hamm sacked for a big loss on second and seventeen, but senior captain and linebacker Ben Krichbaum, who was one of our defensive leaders (he became Massillon's third-all-time-leading tackler, behind Chris Spielman and our very own Coach Leno), missed the tackle on a blitz and Hamm completed a pass for sixteen yards, which kept the drive alive.

"If I would've made that play, they would have had a long fourth down," Ben said. "We called 'New England,' where me and Preston [Hodges] blitz from the same side. Hoban's quarterback was literally right there in front of me, and it should've been the easiest tackle I'd ever make, but I missed, and I was like, 'Shoot, hope I just didn't cost us the game.'"

Hamm took the Knights down the field, and the game came down to this: fourth and six on our nineteen with 2:09 to play. All anyone could think about was what Hoban had done the week before against Mayfield. They were in the same position, and they went for the kill again. We knew they weren't going to go for the game-tying field goal. They were going for the win.

"We ran the exact same blitz that Ben missed on," McConnell said. "I remember [Coach Leno] saying, 'What do you want to do?' I answered, 'I don't want to sit back and let this cat run around. Let's blitz him.' We looked at the script and called 'New England.'"

Preston added: "What's interesting is that we were begging Coach McConnell and Coach Leno to blitz, because we knew it would work. When Ben missed the tackle earlier he kept saying he thought that miss was going to cost us the game. I said, 'Dude, you're alright. The running back is trying to block me. It's literally going to be just you and the quarterback again. The running back is going to block me, the quarterback is going to step up, go make a play.'"

That's exactly what happened. Preston and Ben blitzed from the left side. Preston, on the outside, was picked up by Hoban's running back. Hamm stepped up into the pocket, and before he could even look downfield at a receiver Ben was in his face, at his legs, and brought him down for the sack. Preston was there too, albeit a few seconds later. To his credit, he did fight off the block of Hoban's running back. "I just had to dive in there on the pile to get in on it," Preston said, laughing.

Preston did such a great job of "getting in on it" that he was credited with the tackle from the PA announcer and on TV. But it was Ben.

"Our second half, defensively, was probably the best defensive half I've ever seen a high school team play against a team like that," Coach McConnell said. "The way we stopped them on that fourth-down play was a testament to Ben, Preston, and that entire defense. It goes back to 'Who was leading that defense? Who's holding everybody accountable?' It was Ben and Preston."

We were on our own twenty-two with 2:05 left in the game. Any type of turnover or ineffective series would give the ball back to Hoban. There was no second-guessing: Zion was going to be our guy, period. We needed just one first down to seal the victory. Seems easy, but we *still* didn't have a first down in the entire second half. "Coach Troxler and Coach Mazur both grabbed Zion just before he took the field. Coach Troxler said, 'You better get that damn first down in four plays,'" Zion said, chuckling. "I remember it clear as day because of his Southern accent. You know how he talks."

On first down Aidan handed the ball off to Zion, who busted through the middle for seven yards to the twenty-nine. Three yards to go to slay the giant. We let the clock tick away. The announcer on the telecast said, "I don't think this is hyperbole; this just might be the biggest win in Massillon Football." No pressure or anything. On second down, another handoff to Zion, who was brought down at the thirty. Hoban used its final time-out with 1:14 to go. The stadium reverberated with "T-I-G" and "E-R-S." All of Massillon's fans were on their feet, jumping up and down. Waiting and hoping that the Tigers could pick up two yards. We then used a time-out, just to make sure we had the right play to get it done.

Coach Moore later reflected on that time-out. He said, "We only had a finite amount of time to make our decision. And you know, it probably would've been a great time to call a play action, which may have been wide open, but what if we don't catch it? What if we drop the ball, or we throw the ball high and it's intercepted?"

When our offense got to the sideline, Zion felt there was a calmness. "Coach Moore looked at me in the huddle and said, 'Let's go out there and get that first down. That's what we've been working for.'"

A handoff to Zion up the middle got as close as you could to the thirty-two-yard line. But was it close enough? The refs stopped the clock

Zion began the season wondering if the coaches forgot him. In week thirteen, he got the call for the biggest play of the year.

and brought out the chains. A first down seals the win; inches short gives us quite a decision to make. The chain gang walked out to the field, planted the first-down marker at the twenty-two, and stretched out the chains. The ref made the signal heard around the world: FIRST DOWN!

Coach Moore said, "We played the percentages and ran the ball. I don't make a lot of calls, but this is the way I remember it. They were going to be overplaying on our run formation on one side. We were going to have our fullback on the same side as our running back, and power to that side is our No. 1 play. We went with our No. 1 play, our bread and butter. Zion took that ball and stumbled for the first down, and that was it."

Photo courtesy of JimTrussell on YouTube

The roar of the crowd: Massillon fans unleash a thunderous roar as the refs signal first down. Check it out on YouTube!

The Massillon Tigers beat Archbishop Hoban. The crowd erupted. The Tiger fans screamed with joy. You could feel the steel stadium practically buckle under the stomping feet of the Tiger fans. We did it. We took down Hoban.

Months later, Coach Moore was still shaking his head thinking about that moment. He said, "You know what's funny? We only had one first down in the second half. Zion picked up our only first down of the second half. Then we took a knee to run the clock out."

To illustrate the intense defensive battle in the second half, each team had the ball six times, and here were the results of possessions for each team in the third and fourth quarters: Massillon: punt, punt, punt, punt, downs, end of game. Hoban: punt, punt, punt, punt, fumble, downs.

Hoban coach Tim Tyrrell showed a lot of class after the game. "I told [Coach Moore] after the game, 'Now go win it,'" Tyrrell told *The Independent*. "This shouldn't be the end of it. They've got to go win their first state [playoff] championship. We respect the heck out of their program."

Robbie Page, our senior defensive back, said he knew we were going to win. It wasn't about being cocky; it was about being prepared. "I had all the confidence in the world we were going to win the game, after last year losing to them in the championship, because of the way we prepared—not only that week but through the year," he said. "We had that loss in our head, and nothing was going to get in our way. We knew we would see Hoban again, but this time it would be a different outcome. That whole summer we worked like we never worked before, and it showed in the twelve games before the Hoban game, with no games really close in score. We were coming for vengeance."

Photo by Rocky Dorsey

Manny McElroy is overcome with emotion as the win sets in.

Much praise has to go to the unsung heroes of this cold November night: junior kicker Alex Bauer, junior backup quarterback and holder Zach Catrone, and sophomore snapper Dominic Salvino. They all played a large part in getting us the three points that toppled the dynasty of Hoban.

Dom Salvino had become a very important member of the team early in the season when he was thrust into the position because of an injury to senior Corey Campbell. We called up Dom, who had no experience but was ready because of his hard work and determination. I don't say any of that just because his dad, Paul, is the superintendent of Massillon schools. No, I wouldn't promote my boss and his son for the sake of, um, what's the expression I'm looking for, oh, "sucking up." Seriously, Dom is a wonderful student of mine, and I was proud of his work throughout the season.

"I had prepared myself since the eighth grade for this opportunity, and I was thinking how everything happens for a reason," Dom said. "Me, Zach, and Alex were put on that field for a reason, and together we were able to help us win that game. It was the most amazing feeling to help our team win that game."

I asked Mike Stone, who coaches our kicking and H-backs units, to tell me about those kids. "Let me talk about one of the most underappreciated aspects of football and which is the most important part of special teams, which is your extra-point and field-goal team," he said. "And that includes more than just the kicker; it includes your short snapper and your holder. We had Dom step in, and he had been doing a good job when he was a freshman, so he had earned the trust of the coaching staff when we needed him. I don't believe he had a bad snap all year, at least during games. The one thing you don't realize is how much time those guys spend working on getting it perfect."

Zach added: "I always tell Alex, 'You do this every day. This is just another rep.' And for me, it's usually just trying to do my job to the best of my ability, which is get the ball down in time for him. My job is to make his job easy, so I really just tell myself, 'Just do it to the best of your ability, get the job done, and trust that Alex will make the field goal or extra point.'"

It wasn't always that simple, however.

"During week nine, Coach Jarvis switched up the snap count for field goals from one to two, because teams were starting to jump on the one count," Alex said. "It took me like a couple of weeks to get used to it."

Alex said that after we scored our first touchdown, it looked like Hoban was figuring out the timing. "On our first extra point, Number 19 [Ja'Sean Cogbum] came off the left edge and almost blocked it. So before the field goal attempt I had to make sure I sped things up, to make sure I didn't get it blocked."

Because Alex was thinking about that, he started too early on the field goal attempt and was called for a false start, which backed us up. Alex had missed that first attempt, but because he was whistled for the penalty before the snap, it didn't count, and he got another shot.

"I didn't really care," he said. "It really didn't faze me at all. I knew I was going to make it, because I was a little more relaxed. I knew I missed the field goal, and even though I false-started and we were moved back five yards, I knew I was getting another chance. That relaxed me, so when we lined up again, I nailed it."

We had two chances to get in a circle after the game. We gathered to do our push-ups of course, but we also gathered for the trophy ceremony. We were presented the Division II Region 5 championship trophy. It felt like we had conquered the world, but we still had two more games to play—hopefully. The team boarded the buses and drove through downtown Massillon, just like after the McKinley game. Who knows how fast everyone else drove from Akron to Massillon to be waiting there for us? The kids stuck their hands out the bus windows and high-fived the town. Massillon was 13-0, and we were on our way.

Terrance rushed for eighty-seven yards on seventeen carries. Zion had sixty yards. Terrance sat out the end of the game with bruised ribs and an injured ankle, and we were unsure what next week would bring for him. He was carrying the world on his shoulders. Zion was there to back him up. Just like a Tiger should.

Eli, Becca, and Nate Moore flank Zion and equipment aide La Tyvia Henderson as they sing the alma mater after the win.

THE SCORE BOARD

Teams	Q1	Q2	Q3	Q4	F
Massillon Tigers (13-0)	14	3	0	0	17
Akron Hoban (11-2)	7	7	0	0	14

Chapter 20
Avon Eagles

With everything Terrance had to go through leading up to and during the Hoban game, we all knew that physically, and mentally, he probably wasn't going to be ready to play against Avon, and he wasn't. Against Hoban, Terrance hurt his ankle and ribs. Our medical staff informed us that Terrance wasn't going to be ready for the Avon game. The media was still asking questions about Terrance's legal issues. Coach Moore would not talk to anyone about the situation, nor did he allow any of the players or coaches to speak about it, because it was all about focusing on Avon. Eagles Head Coach Mike Elder was well respected and ran a disciplined, quality program. We had a lot of respect for him, his staff, and his team, and vice versa. "[Massillon] is just crazy about football," he said. "They get tremendous support. I've tried to explain to our players the passion that city has for the game of football and how they'll travel well. It will be a hostile environment, and we'll embrace that. I want our kids to be prepared for it."

Without Terrance in the backfield, it was once again time for our guy Zion to step up. Zion had been amazing for us all year, and whenever we called on him to step up he delivered.

Just about all of Massillon drove to Parma to see if their Tigers could make it to back-to-back state championship games for the first time.

Zion deserved an award for human spirit. He knew he wasn't going to be the No. 1 back when the season started, so he asked how he could help in other ways. He did it all for us all season with a "yes sir, no sir" mentality, and that didn't change when we needed his leadership against Avon in the playoffs. He had come through with that big first-down run against Hoban the week before to seal the victory, and we were going to need many more of those first-down runs against Avon.

All Zion did was rush twenty times for a game-high 146 yards and four touchdowns in Terrance's absence, leading us to a 35-10 win.

"I knew I had to step up and become a big player in that game," Zion said. "I put the team on my shoulders knowing we lost the state championship the year before and that we were one game away from getting there again. I wanted to make sure I did all the little things right against Avon . . . all the little things that were best for the team. I put my head down and just went to work."

Avon was a wounded warrior in that game. Their starting quarterback was out. Joey Lance, who had played receiver all year, stepped in to play QB. He was hard to bring down and led Avon on a seventy-eight-yard touchdown march in the second quarter. The Tigers were too much for

Avon, but Lance's performance was something to see. He played with heart and never quit. They were an admirable adversary.

Avon scored all ten of its points in the first half. Our defense hadn't given up a single point in the second half in any of the playoff games.

We'd done it. We were going back to the state championship game. The mantra had worked. We would once again get to play that fifteenth game. The hard work that had started way back in the off-season in January was paying huge dividends. Here we were in late November. We had gone 14-0 for the second straight season.

Our players hugged one another and celebrated. Coach J. P. Simon, who had helped to spearhead 15 for 15, blew his whistle and the team surrounded him. As the players and cheerleaders, students, and some football fans dropped to the ground to give him fifteen, the large crowd chanted out the numbers at peak volume. One hundred teenagers had set a goal, and it had come true. We knew the state game would be a challenge. Our opponent, we soon learned, was Cincinnati La Salle.

First they sing, then they count. The team performs after beating Avon.

Terrance missing the Avon game was just a microcosm of the type of season he had had. Whenever it looked like things were going well, he had to face adversity. And when he seemed like he was back on track, there was always another roadblock. I felt bad for him. At first I didn't understand how he managed to cope with all that adversity. But then, months later, it all made sense, his uncanny ability to remain tranquil throughout his turbulent year at Massillon, because of a writing-workshop assignment he turned in to me late in the 2020 school year. I had encouraged my students to think deep and write even deeper. I gave them this quote for the assignment:

"*Yea though I walk through the Valley of the Shadow of Death, I shall fear no evil, for I am the scariest, meanest person in the Valley.*" — General George S. Patton

These were the instructions: "Tell me about one time that you were not afraid because you had courage, felt prepared and confident that you would succeed, and believed in yourself like, 'I got this!' (250 words)."

I gave this assignment to my students while we were in the middle of remote learning in early May 2020 due to the COVID-19 stay-at-home order. When I read what Terrance had turned in, I could feel the mental anguish he had gone through during his year with us. I also felt his sense of triumph and victory because of his commitment and relationship with the Lord.

Here is the assignment he wrote, verbatim:

A time in my life when I was 100% confident in myself is when I transferred here to Massillon. Everybody said that I wouldn't start and this would not be the place for me and this and that but Coach Morgan nobody understood the off-season work I put in going into my senior year. I worked my tail off. So what people on the outside was saying didn't matter because I had already put my time in and paid my dues so I already knew what I was capable of doing because of my drive and determination to be great. And most importantly I had God on my side, and when I say that I worked so hard during the off-season, I wasn't just talking about physically, but spiritually also. So this is how it played out- so I found out I was coming here so I knew I had to work hard to get what I wanted. That's obvious. But I wanted to get baptized heading into the biggest year of my high school career in the mix of everybody throwing dirt on my name because I knew once I did that nobody couldn't mess with me. I was covered in the blood of Jesus and still when adversity hit me I wasn't worried. I had no fear because I knew it was just the devil trying to get at me. Everything was going great for me the whole season. I was on my way to my first high school championship.

But before that, everyone remembers when they came and got me from school. The devil didn't like me getting baptized and me having the best season of my high school career. He didn't like that at all. So he tried to strike and God allowed him just to show him that he can try to bring the child of God down and that it may work at first but in the long run it won't because I believe God lets the battle last a little longer between him and Satan just to show Satan will never come out on top.

And I say that because I'm still fighting my case but some people don't know that. But all this is a part of my journey and testimony. God puts his strong angels through the harder battles in life. My life has been a little rough going through this little incident and then finding out I have to go to a junior college. But I don't look at it as a bad thing. I look at it as being a few steps behind doesn't necessarily mean failure, sometimes God is preparing me for a great launch."

I was so proud of what Terrance wrote. It was simply beautiful.

He got an A+.

THE SCORE BOARD

Teams	Q1	Q2	Q3	Q4	F
Massillon Tigers (14-0)	7	14	7	7	35
Avon Eagles (13-1)	7	3	0	0	10

Chapter 21
Cincinnati La Salle
(State Championship)

In many ways, the 15-for-15 mantra reminds me of when Babe Ruth called his home run as he walked up to bat in the 1932 World Series. The Massillon Tiger players pointed in the direction of the state championship way back in January: "We will play fifteen games. We will arrive at the state championship. We will hit that home run." And we did it. The coaches supported the brazen move. Our team and town got swept up in the gesture. T-shirts were sold, hashtags were born, and there were a whole lot of people counting along to fifteen in 2019. Whether the tradition will continue in 2020 or not, I don't know. In back-to-back years the team, led by quarterback Aidan Longwell, circled a date on the calendar and kept that appointment. Aidan won the Stark County MVP award. He, and the senior class, had won more games than any other Massillon class.

Throughout the playoffs, Coach Weber continued sending letters to the team. I deliberately haven't sampled the playoff letters, so that his final message could have more of an impact. As always, Coach Weber's devotion to the players, the town, and the mystique of Massillon is evident in his words. Here is his fifteenth letter of 2019.

Coach Weber's "Words of Wisdom"

What a journey this is. What a ride that will conclude tonight. Make no mistake, this isn't a letter that is going to reminisce. Reminisce about what? The first 14 weeks? Those are over. There is one thing left to do. The Warpath of this season ends after that, and we can do all of the hugging and remembering we want to. Not now. We have a mission to accomplish. A goal to reach. There is only one goal in this town. ONE GOAL. A State Championship.

There are a lot of things that are coming to a confluence tonight. An apex. A crescendo. Tonight, the City of Massillon, Massillon High School student body and teachers/administrators, coaches, players, and thousands upon thousands of rabid loyal diehard fans will all come together at the right moment in time. A crescendo is a steady increase in force or intensity and is the climactic point or moment in such an increase; peak. Crescendo is a term usually associated with music. When an orchestra whose parts are working as separate sounds to weave together a piece of music, all at once, for a moment come together to a peak for a dramatic effect, they create a crescendo. A crescendo is not sustained. It is a moment. All it can be is a moment because of the intensity. Individually each element I listed earlier has its own individual importance. Our great city. The most perfect high school anyone could ever ask for. A set of EDMF administrators, coaches and players, and the best, most intense fans at any level, in this country. Tonight, we all will see and feel the coming together of all the pieces. For 48 minutes, we will all peak together as one.

This game is being played for all of us. The responsibility before you is great. You are the hopes and dreams of a town. A town that is tough. So tough. This town and its people have endured so much since the 1970's when the jobs slowly started to leave. But the town stayed intact. Our population has not changed over all this time. Why? Because of you. Because of the Tigers. You keep this town together. People in town pinning their hopes and dreams on you is a huge responsibility to put on a teenager. But it's what we do. It is what we have always done. Tonight is so important to so many people. You included. Tonight is your moment. Once in a lifetime moment that will come and go. There is only one outcome that is acceptable. I have lived through as a player, the other outcome. After the game, the booster club gave us a State Runner-Up t-shirt. I've never put it on my body. The state gave us a shiny state runner-up plaque. I've never hung it. We have one goal in this town. Anything else and we have great memories, good times remembered. But there will be a hole.

We will do this. Together. All of us. For each other. The team, the town, the school, the coaches, and Tiger Nation. For 48 minutes, starting at 7:00, we will reach a crescendo together.

One mind. One body. One team. One town. We are Massillon!

Have no doubts. Have no fears. You are the ones. We are Massillon.

Go Tigers!!! Beat Cincinnati La Salle!!! Be State Champions!!!

After the Avon win, and our brief postgame celebration on the field and in the locker room, the hour-or-so bus ride back to Massillon was quite satisfying. We had stayed the course, didn't look ahead, knocked off Warren Harding, Hoban, Perry, and now Avon, and everything was there in front of us. Everything we, and other teams before us, wished and hope for was right there in front of us. We were about to play in our second-straight state championship game. You might think there was unbearable pressure on us, but there wasn't. Really there wasn't, and it was because it came from the top, from Coach Moore.

The coaches got a group message from Coach Moore that we were having a staff meeting at 11:30 a.m. on Sunday. We met in Coach Moore's office and it was laid back as always, with Coach McConnell roasting Coach Jarvis, or Coach Simon roasting Coach Leno, or Coach Stone roasting Coach McConnell, or Coach Hackenbracht roasting EVERYONE. Coach Moore was sitting behind his desk, leaning back in his chair, with the rest of us scattered in chairs and couches along the wall. Once we settled down, the first thing Coach Moore said was, "Hey, guys, let's not go into practice with the this-is-for-all-the-marbles kind of do-or-die attitude. Let's just go into this like it's just another game. Let's just go into it like it's only another week, week fifteen."

In all honesty, Coach Moore didn't have to worry about that, because nothing had ever changed for us during practice, from week one to week fifteen. It was always the same. We were focused but loose. Always. Don't get me wrong, Coach Moore and the rest of the staff, myself included, would not hold back if we felt guys were taking plays off or not focusing, but that didn't happen often. Think about this: many of our players had played forty-three games in three years. Teams that didn't make the playoffs those years had played only thirty. Our seniors had played thirteen more games. Think about the practices and extra reps that go along with those extra thirteen games. Now think of all the additional practice reps for each starter and nonstarter that went along with those extra thirteen games. Our guys had completed so many reps, even the young kids on the scout team.

Game preparation then started. The school that Coach Moore had coached at before Massillon was this week's opponent, Cincinnati La Salle. He was the head coach there from 2013 to 2014. He won the

Coach Moore talks to his team during practice in the indoor facility.

Division II state championship in 2014. However, that never was a topic of discussion, because Coach Moore had been at Massillon for five years, and his heart, and home, was Massillon.

On Monday during the school day, Preston Hodges came into my room. This wasn't unusual; players whom I didn't have for class often stopped in to chat for a few minutes. We started talking about the state championship game and what it would mean to win. Preston started talking about a state championship ring. I said, "Let's say we won . . . and Preston, I ain't looking ahead and you *better* not be either, but if we won, would you wear it all the time?" He said, "No. But I would if it had Obie [the mascot] on it. I would want it right on top, so when I'm talking to people I can flash it." I laughed then said, "I'm not talking about this anymore. We gotta focus. Go to class!" Preston was laughing and started walking out of my room. He then turned around and said, "Coach Morgan, one thing . . . " I said, "What?" He said, "If you visualize it, it will happen." My eyes lit up. I looked at him so intensely and didn't say a word. I was almost in amazement at what he said, because it was so introspective. I just nodded my head in agreement as he walked out. He made a great point. He wasn't being cocky; he was confident because of the way we prepared him and the rest of the team as a coaching staff.

I went home and told Jill about the conversation I had with Preston, and she said, "David, it's just faith. He has faith in you guys, himself, and his teammates. That's all he's saying, and I agree with him. You guys are going to do this."

The week was full of hope and flashes of wondering what it would be like. How would the town react to finally winning a state championship on the field? It had been forty-nine years. Everywhere you went, people talked about it. The thing I noticed was that no one was saying they wanted to win for themselves. It was always, "I want my father to see them win while he is still here" or "I want to experience the win with my daughter, my son . . . with my family." That is what it was all about. Family. Legacy. History. With just one more game, an entire town's dream could come true. It was too much to think about. It came into our minds for a moment, and then it was brushed away to keep the task at hand in perfect focus.

Day of the State Championship Game

Because of Coach Moore's mantra of "normalcy," our practices and demeanor all week were just that: normal. I'm sure we all had our individual feelings and visions of what it would be like to win a state championship—the first in the playoff era for Massillon—but it wasn't talked about (outside of my conversation with Preston).

On the day of the game, Thursday, December 5, 2019, I walked over to the stadium to do one of my regular jobs on game day for the last time ever, which was to write the game itinerary on the board. Every game during the season I had followed a routine. School ended at 2:15 p.m. I would pack up my things and head down to the cafeteria, where the players and coaches would be served our pregame meal by the Tiger Moms. I'd grab a plate of whatever delicious food was being served and sit at one of the tables with some of the players to small-talk and joke.

Today would be a little different. I didn't hang around the cafeteria. I wanted to get to the stadium early, and it wasn't because I was "Mr. Serious." I think I just knew the finality of this unforeseen journey—win or lose—that I had been on for the past fourteen weeks.

As I left the cafeteria and made my way to the stadium, the December sun jabbed me (it was in the midforties) with a warm, gentle barrage of rays. There was nothing but sun, and silence. It was as if everyone within a five-mile radius was purposely keeping quiet. It was eerie. Usually on my walk over I would hear

Photo by Kenny Roda - 1480 WHBC

The captains prepare to take the field.

The Pro Football Hall of Fame can be seen behind the La Salle fans,
as the Tigers run out on the field for their final game of 2019.

music blaring from the parking lot adjacent to the stadium, where our players had parked their cars, or music emanating from the locker room before I even got to the entrance. Not today.

When I walked into the locker room there were players already there, but I didn't get the customary "What's up, Coach Milk Dud?!!" That was an affectionate name the guys came up with for me because I am black and I do shave my caramel-colored head bald, making it look like a Milk Dud.

There was nothing. No greeting. The guys had their headphones on, focusing, not paying any attention to what or who was around them. You could hear the squeak of the marker as I posted times for the game, which would be my very last experience as a coach inside the team locker room at Paul Brown Tiger Stadium. It was a surreal moment for me. It was moving. I had this overwhelming feeling of "Man, whether we win or not, do you know what the hell you just experienced coaching here? This was once in a lifetime, dude." It wasn't like Coach Moore had specifically said I was going to be the running backs coach for just one year, but I knew it. There were a ton of coaches out there more qualified than I was for this dream job. I was one and done. And it was getting close to done. I kept writing, and squeaking, and honor and pride filled my heart. I felt almost a calming presence surrounding me. I don't know what it was, but it seemed to speak to me. It said, "It's OK. You are where you're supposed to be. You needed to experience this."

There were more than 11,000 fans at Tom Benson Hall of Fame Stadium, and it was time to fulfill our destiny. There was something sweet about it being at the same spot as the Massillon-McKinley game. That day was the best day. But today could be even better. There wasn't any pregame Knute Rockne type of motivational speech by Coach Moore. Back at Paul Brown Tiger Stadium, Coach Moore had held a brief team meeting, which we always do, home or away. It was about the kids focusing on the jobs they had to do, and nothing else. On Sunday, the first thing Coach Moore had told us in our staff meeting was to keep everything as normal as possible and not get too uptight about the game. It was hard, but we did our best.

La Salle got the opening kickoff, and our defense held the Lancers, forcing a three-and-out series. After La Salle's punt, our offense marched right down the field, just as we had scripted. We got down to the Lancers' five-yard-line and faced a third-and-goal situation. Aidan tossed a pass to Jayden Ballard, but it fell incomplete. We had to settle for a twenty-one-yard field goal by Alex Bauer with 8:39 left in the first quarter to take a 3-0 lead. We felt good about how our defense had stopped La Salle and how we showed the ability to move the ball downfield against a stout defense.

However, La Salle's offense was more efficient on its second drive. The Lancers started at their own twenty-three with 8:37 left in the opening quarter. In six plays and seventy-seven yards, they scored on a six-yard run, and our early lead evaporated into a 7-3 deficit. I heard Coach Mazur say in my headset, "It's OK, let's just get it back. No worries."

On the first play of the second quarter, we had the ball first and ten at our eleven. Terrance took the handoff from Aidan and was hit at the line of scrimmage and fumbled. It was uncharacteristic of not just Terrance but our entire backfield to cough up the football, but in this, the biggest game in the history of the program, we wound up fumbling three times.

La Salle recovered with great field position. It took the Lancers just three plays to score and take a 14-3 lead. Coach Stone, who always sat next to me in the press box, didn't say anything, but let out a huge sigh.

He knew we couldn't give a great team like this easy opportunities to score.

We didn't let the game get away from us, however. Our offense responded with a quick score, needing just four plays to cut the lead to 14-10 thanks to a thirty-eight-yard touchdown pass from Aidan Longwell to Jayden Ballard with 8:42 left in the second quarter.

We needed a stop. The Lancers marched deep into our territory, but we forced them into a third-and-eight situation at our nineteen with less than seven minutes to go before halftime. However, La Salle quarterback Zach Branam delivered, hitting Jake Seibert on a ten-yard reception for the first down. A play later, the Lancers went ahead 21-10.

We got the ball back with 5:59 before the break—plenty of time to mount a drive. But our offense stalled, so we had to punt. La Salle couldn't do anything with the ball either, so they punted back to us. There was 1:20 left to play in the half.

Coach Mazur remained calm. I remember him saying, through the headset, "OK, we're alright, guys. Let's just get a touchdown and regroup in the locker room."

He was talking to himself, but talking to everyone. And everyone must have been listening, because our offense responded once again. On our first play, Aidan tossed a sixty-nine-yard touchdown pass to Jayden, cutting the lead to 21-17 heading into the locker room.

During halftime, we let the players talk among themselves, so that they could self-analyze what had happened on the field and figure out what adjustments needed to be made. The coaching staff met in the large coaches' locker-room area, with the offensive coaches in one section and the defensive coaches in another. A clock in the room displayed the same time as the game clock on the field, so we knew exactly how much time we had to strategize as a staff before gathering the players to discuss adjustments. We made our plan. We were fourteen and a half weeks into the season. We weren't going to rewrite the playbook. We hadn't surrendered a single score in the second half during the entire playoffs. All we needed was to play Tiger football. Hold them and score once. If we did that, all our dreams would come true.

Once the second half started, the difference in the game was our inability to hold onto the football. It reminded me of what Coach Jim Tressel told me when I asked him for advice after I accepted the job as running backs coach. He gave me one bit of advice to pass on to my running backs: "Ball control."

Zion fumbled on our own thirty-seven midway through the third quarter, and La Salle responded with a ten-play scoring drive, giving the Lancers a comfortable 28-10 lead with 1:46 left in the quarter. La Salle tacked on two field goals and outscored us 13-0 in the second half.

Final score: La Salle 34, Massillon 17.

Our dream of 15 for 15 was shattered. We had lost only two games in two years, and they were both the state championship. The one game Massillon had never won. We had put in the work, but the prize was still out there.

Coach Moore told Chris Easterling of *The Independent*: "First thing's first, you have to give credit to La Salle. They're a great football team and played a great ballgame. They put us in some tough spots, so you have to give them a lot of credit."

All year we had had a solid running game; against La Salle, it was held in check. Zion was our leading rusher, with fifty-eight yards on ten

Their faces say it all: center Cole Jones and quarterback Aidan Longwell hold the trophies for runner-up in the Division II State game.

carries. The Lancers didn't allow Terrance to break any of his signature big runs. He was held to just sixteen yards on seven carries. Aidan actually had more yards (twenty-nine) rushing than Terrance. I really do think he was still battling the rib injury he had sustained in the game against Hoban in the regional championship, which had forced him to sit out the semifinal game against Avon. I also believe that after the arrest, he just wasn't the same runner. Who could be?

Meanwhile, La Salle quarterback Zach Branam had an outstanding game. He finished with a game-high 166 yards rushing and carried the ball twenty-two times, which was astounding. Gi'Bran Payne finished with 133 yards on eighteen carries with a touchdown, and Cam Porter had fifty-seven yards on eighteen carries. Those three players were dominant and helped La Salle control the game on the ground.

"We struggled getting off blocks, especially with the outside zone," Coach Moore told sportswriter Ryan Isley of cleveland.com. "[The La Salle offensive line] is a group that plays hard, and you have to give them a lot of credit. We just didn't do a good enough job tonight."

Isley also gave us some love in his article. "This was the fifth time since the OHSAA's playoff era began in 1972 that Massillon had reached the state championship game only to come up short, and the second season in a row in which the Tigers finished as the Division II runners-up. Despite not winning a championship in the 47 years of the playoff era, Massillon still has one of the most loyal fan bases in all of Ohio and the sea of orange and black filled the home stands of the stadium."

"It is really humbling, and as a program we are very appreciative of the support we do have," Moore said. "That's one of the really tough parts. We really wanted to deliver that [championship] to the city of Massillon tonight, and we fell short."

Former Tiger Ellery Moore, who was in the booth next to me calling the game on the radio said, "The loss to La Salle was the biggest disappointment because we slayed the dragon of Hoban. We took out the leader of the pack for four years, and then we ran into another opponent that no one talked about, and they were better than Hoban. They were better than Hoban was in 2018. They had a very well-oiled machine, and they were just better than us that day."

Coach Stone, who is "Mr. Analytics," summed up the game perfectly:

"I thought we started out great. Not getting the touchdown hurt, but I think what hurt more than that and what really shifted the momentum was when we turned the ball over deep in our own territory on the first play of the second quarter and us down 7-3. They scored two plays later and went up 14-3. Football isn't really a tricky sport. When you look at it, it comes down to three major statistics; turnovers, explosive plays, and missed tackles, and we lost all three of those against La Salle. When you lose all three of those, your chances of winning are less than 10 percent. Another thing is we usually have eight to ten explosive plays in the run game, and they did a really good job of limiting those."

After the game, as you would expect, there were tears. Tears because of the hurt. All the work, commitment, and energy expended, just for it to end this way. A second consecutive loss in the state championship was heartbreaking, and for the seniors the hurt went even deeper, because those guys had experienced losing in the state championship twice, and would never get another shot. They would go down in the history books as the most successful class in Massillon's extraordinary football history, but even with most games played, most games won, and more, they didn't get the one thing they wanted most—the title.

It took time for us coaches who work from the press box to get down to the field after the game. We went straight to the coaches' office. The locker room was empty, because everyone was still on the field. I heard the sound of a child crying. Curled up in a corner was Ella Moore, Nate's daughter. She was sobbing. I hadn't had the time to process that we lost. I had been in game mode. Hearing the sniffles of a young child made it start to set in. This loss was going to affect everyone in Massillon, from the oldest fan to the youngest. I headed out to the field to congratulate La Salle, as well as our own guys for putting together a hell of a season, even in defeat.

Once we all left the field, the players filed into the locker room, and the coaches headed over to the coaches' area. It was quiet, but we could hear the muffled sounds of crying resonating throughout the locker room. Then Nate said, "Should we go downtown?" He was referring to the ritual of us riding through downtown, streets blocked off and fans everywhere, as we got off the buses to mingle with the crowd, like we did after the McKinley game and the subsequent playoffs wins. No one said a word in response, but we all reacted. Everyone shook their heads no.

Becca Moore popped her head into the room and said, "Just so you know, there are people down there waiting for you guys."

The coaches left the office and went into the locker room. Coach Moore had some of the seniors speak. The players were all down on one knee in a circle. Manny McElroy was first.

"For my seniors, this is it, man. Y'all played y'all asses off and y'all did. I saw it. I played my ass off, too. And to our juniors and younger guys coming up, you guys have to play your asses off, too. You gotta trust it, man. You gotta trust the coaches. Keep playing. Keep working hard. I love every single one of you."

Then the team responded as they always do when a senior speaks after the game: "Manny, three claps."

(Clap, Clap, Clap!)

Starting defensive end Corey Campbell said, "Juniors who are about to be seniors, when y'all are in the weight room and y'all see somebody slacking off, excuse my language but get on their asses. It's the little stuff that will matter. Look, just go be great next year."

The team in unison, "Corey, three claps."

(Clap, Clap, Clap!)

Zion Phifer, my running back, whom I loved for his spirit and Tiger heart, went next, "Like Corey was saying, juniors, y'all will do this again

The captains and Coach Moore meet the press after the loss.

next year. You see us crying. It hurts. It was our last year, so next year you gotta go out there and give 110 percent every play. I apologize for my fumble. Maybe that could've been our turnaround."

The team: "Zion, three claps."

(Clap, Clap, Clap!)

Zion left the circle and got back on one knee. Coach Moore asked if any coaches had anything to say. Coach Troxler stepped into the circle.

"Seniors, thank you for what you've done for this program. It was a great two-year run, and for some of you a great three-year run. Like Corey said, to be elite you can't take reps off in the weight room. You can't have down days in the weight room. And some of you younger guys, it's time to grow up. We're going to take that next step. Let's get it done in the weight room, and again, seniors, thank you. I love you guys, I'm proud of you, and you hold your damn heads up . . . HOLD YOUR HEADS UP! Be proud of what you accomplished, because we sure as hell are."

Before the team could give Coach Troxler his customary three claps, Manny stepped back up to speak to the team, in reference to Zion blaming the loss on his fumble. We had fumbled three times and lost all three, and two of those happened deep in our own territory and resulted in La Salle touchdowns. La Salle played a flawless game. They did not have any turnovers.

"I just want to say one more thing . . . I know Zion just said he apologized for his fumble, but if anybody in here feels that the game could've been different because you made a mistake, don't think that. I said this the other day at touchdown club: I would take anybody in this room over anybody else on this day, any day of the week. I count on you guys, and I know you guys count on me. Don't let that ruin you, bro. Please don't. You guys are so much better than the one mistake you made."

The team: "Manny, three claps."

(Clap, Clap, Clap!)

The locker room remained silent as Superintendent Paul "Sal" Salvino, a former Tiger player himself, spoke.

"I know you guys are hurting. But don't lose sight of the fact that we had a packed house, and this ride that you've been on all year, and for some of you seniors three years, has changed lives in our city. Our whole city has been uplifted by all you men on this team and the men on this coaching staff. The whole damn city has been uplifted by the spirit and the fight of this program from you guys and all these seniors. I know it sucks. I know it hurts. It's going to hurt, and it should hurt. I'm so proud of you guys; the whole city is so proud of you guys. There are going to be people who want to hug you, talk to you, and thank you. Listen to them and let them, because you deserve it, because of all the sacrifices you made—the fifteen-week grind, the grind that started back in January, and for you young cats that means the grind starts again next month. I love you and thank you for everything."

The team: "Coach Sal, three claps."

(Clap, Clap, Clap!)

Coach Moore stepped between kneeling players to the middle of the circle. As he made his way, all you could hear was sniffling and stifled crying from players.

"Number one, this hurts, and things like this are supposed to hurt, and it hurts because you put so much into it. You laid it on the line, and you laid it on the line not for fifteen weeks, but since January 3. You risked it all, but sometimes things like this happen. It's part of life. Now, the question moving forward is how are you guys going to respond to this? Don't lose sight of everything that you guys put into it along the way, the process, how you guys improved as a team. How you improved as individuals, and how you grew as a person. And you can't do that unless you're willing to risk it all, and you guys did that. I'm so proud of this group. I'm so proud of this senior class. I love being with you guys. Seniors, I'm going to miss the hell out of you. You've been an unbelievable group. You set the standard. You set the bar for how things are supposed to be done. You guys are Tigers, man, and I love you. Let's get a break."

Months later, after having more time to reflect, Coach Moore said, "I remember telling all the coaches I was proud of them. It was a heartbreaking moment, especially when you've gone fifteen weeks. It's like somebody died, because you've got this team of a hundred guys, coaches, and support staff, and even though you're going to have a team next year, it's never going to be that same team together, ever again. So when you have reached that point of finality, that is so heavy by itself to deal with—the fact that you didn't hit that ultimate goal. It's a really, really emotional time. You feel for everybody as a head coach, but as a leader you have to set the tone of how to handle that situation and how to start to turn the page, and that was tough."

For Coach Moore, the passing of the months only reinforced his determination to win a state championship. "Going fifteen weeks is hard mentally, physically, and emotionally. What our kids and coaches did was amazing; however, the disappointment . . . that is something that still sticks with our staff and players. It's going to drive us to get back and finish. I truly believe if we can get back, we can win it. I did feel really bad for guys like Aidan Longwell, Preston Hodges, Cole Jones, Manny McElroy, Ben Krichbaum, Robbie Paige, and Luke Murphy, just to name a few. Those guys worked so freaking hard and got their hearts ripped out week fifteen. That's what's going to drive all of us in 2020—that endless chase for perfection!"

Coach Weber, who always had the right words, is someone I looked to for clarity in these moments of disappointment. When the season was long over, I asked him to reflect on the moment of knowing that we had fallen short of our goal. He said, "As the clock ticked to

Photo by Rocky Dorsey

Warrior with a heart of gold: Senior DL Manny McElroy hugs Nathan Forte.

zero, and we began to make our way across the field to shake hands with our opponent, whether it was this year or last year, there was a feeling of just utter disappointment. Most players and coaches never have an opportunity to play in the state championship. We had two, back-to-back opportunities. We weren't able to win either one, and the disappointment that comes with that is not really a 'We wanted to win, but didn't,' competition type of disappointment. There was normal disappointment for the kids who worked so hard, and our coaches who did the same. The biggest disappointment, however, that always comes over me after a regular-season loss, after a playoff loss, or after a state-championship loss is the disappointment I feel for the people behind me in the stands. Those people travel with us anywhere we go, because football in Massillon is important, for all of us. The people in those stands are the reason that we are allowed as a program to be who we are. Because they support that. They want this kind of program, and they demand a certain outcome from this program. Our fans don't want us to win. Everyone's fans want them to win. Our fans demand it. And they hold up their end every Friday or Saturday. I looked at the stands prior to the game and a couple times during the game. I would turn around and see the sea of humanity there for us, living through us. My disappointment in the moments after the game was mostly for them. As teams and coaching staff come and go, those people are always the constant that make us who we are."

I will never be disappointed in Coach Weber. He is as much of a hero to me as he is to all our kids.

Ellery Moore, who can rival Weber with inspiring words, couldn't help but think about the loss and the kids months later. He said, "Aidan Longwell is the greatest Massillon quarterback I have ever seen with my own two eyes. To do what he did for the program, and be there two times in a row, and fall short both times, it's gonna sting a little bit more because he was the leader. I remember being the leader of the 1999 Tigers. We went undefeated and we lost to Perry. And I hold that in my heart to this day. I was supposed to lead us to success and I didn't. So Aidan is gonna hurt the most. I think he is the greatest of all time. As I sit and think of that loss, it shows you that competing against the parochial schools is pretty heavy. It was a tough loss. It gives me goosebumps thinking about how our defense played above their level all year, until that game. La Salle was more athletic. They were faster. We ran into someone who was flat out better than we were. Was I disappointed that we lost? Yes. Am proud of that team? You bet. The loss doesn't diminish their legacy. The only way to diminish their legacy is if the town forgets what these kids did. Even if we win the state championship in 2021, we can't forget what they have done for all of us. This team's legacy lives on."

On the night of that game against La Salle, as we gathered in the locker room and debated about whether to go downtown, Becca Moore had been right, as she always was.

As the buses drove into downtown Massillon, there were more fans waiting to congratulate us than there were for any of the previous playoff games. Thousands of smiling, cheering faces. They were chanting. They were clapping. I wiped away the condensation on my window. I could see faces for just a second as we drove by them. I could see right into their eyes as if I was seeing into their souls for just a flash. I recognized what I saw. I had seen it every week for months. They looked the same as

Photo by Rocky Dorsey

Win or lose. Massillon always. The town greets the team.

they did at the McKinley parade. They were ready to go beat McKinley again. They looked the same as they did at our season opener against St. V. They were ready for next season to start again. I am pretty sure they looked the same as they did the year before, and the year before that and the decade before. They weren't broken. They were born for this. They had been bred for this. It was Tiger Town. It was Massillon, Ohio. Were they sad? You bet. But they weren't giving up. They were just getting started. A few hours after the end of the 2019 season, this group of football fanatics was ready to suit up and do it all over again.

To be honest, I don't know how they do it. I was just ready to go home. See Jill, pet D. J., and start the rest of my life, as a former Massillon Tiger coach—the best sports experience of my life. Go Tigers.

THE SCORE BOARD

Teams	Q1	Q2	Q3	Q4	F
Massillon Tigers (14-1)	3	14	0	0	17
Cincinnati La Salle (13-2)	7	14	7	6	34

Epilogue

I had informed Coach Moore not too long into the season that I was going to write a book about my experience, but that I would not let it interfere with my coaching duties. He was 100 percent supportive. The great thing about Nate Moore is he's authentic. He's got a great heart, he's a family man to the core, and he genuinely cares about people. I didn't really know Nate that well my first few years teaching at Massillon, simply because I didn't interact with him much. He was the athletic director and I was an assistant JV baseball coach. Nate and I were cordial and friendly, but it wasn't until the last two years that I had started to really bond with him. He is a great man, and I'm happy I can call him my friend.

A few weeks after the state championship game, I was sitting in front of the entrance of Akron Children's Hospital waiting for Jill to finish work. We were on Christmas break from school, so I was back to my routine of taking Jill to work. Once we were back in the car, my cell phone rang, and it was Nate.

It felt like the journey had come full circle.

I answered. "Nate, what's up?"

"Nothing much. Hey, I know you wanted to talk after the season, and I just wanted to tell you some things."

With that, Nate started talking, and talking, and talking. I always have my digital recorder and mini notepads with me, because at heart I'll always be a journalist. It was as if Nate wanted to get some things off his chest, in a therapeutic way, and talking to me for the book was his chance to reflect on the 2019 season.

He said that the day after the state championship game, a bunch of our players posted messages on social media thanking people for their support. He mentioned how Aidan had posted a thank-you to the people who talked about how important Massillon football was. But Aidan also posted that he wanted to apologize to the city of Massillon for not bringing home a state championship. Nate said that at the booster club meeting on the Monday following the game, a sweet old lady had raised her hand and commented about Aidan's post. She didn't want Aidan or any of the other players to feel that way.

Nate told me he appreciated her sentiments. "It was a nice thought, and I understood where she was coming from, and even where Aidan was coming from. Then it reminded me how similar that post was to what happened after games when kids wanted to stand up in front of the team and give comments. When a kid wants to stand up and take responsibility for maybe a fumble or dropped pass, it was the other players who said, 'It doesn't matter.'

"I used to basically not let them do that. I would just brush them off, just like that lady. I wanted them to feel like they didn't need to apologize, because they played their hardest. But more recently, over

Photo by Rocky Dorsey

Head Coach Nate Moore smiles at the Avon game.

the last couple of years, I've come to the realization that I think it's a good thing that they did that. I think it's a great example for their teammates. It sets a really good precedent for those in their lives to take accountability for the things they have done, or things they didn't do. I think that's something that's missing from society in many ways. We live in a world where everyone wants to blame everyone else for everything, especially on social media. Everyone points fingers and places blame on everybody. Here's Aidan, a kid who feels like he didn't live up to the standard that was set, and he wants to stand up in front of his team and take accountability for that. I think that's a beautiful thing. I think in a lot of ways those kids have earned that pain. They've earned the right to stand up and take accountability for falling short."

Nate didn't mean these kids failed. "I think there is a powerful lesson in that, and it's a lesson that I think the world needs to hear. There's nothing inherently wrong with how the lady was thinking, but it's unrealistic to think that life is all roses. It's not. And it can't be, and I don't think it should be. I mean, without experiencing pain, do you really know what joy feels like? Can you really see what that's like? I don't think you can. Losing is a wonderful lesson for the kids, and they are handling it correctly. The adults sometimes will want to say, 'Here comes some pain, here comes some discomfort, let's try to avoid that,' but pain is growth. Pain is not the enemy. Pain is a teacher."

I then asked Nate what the greatest football lesson our players learned this year was.

"You know, David, I'd say that pain is not something to be afraid of or run away from. You should embrace the pain and run to the pain, because that's where true growth comes from. Where do kids learn that if it's not athletics? Certainly there's other ways, but man, what an unbelievable laboratory for discovering those truths to life. There's so much that goes into the season. The preparation, all the time we spend together, all the hard work, all the sacrifice for something beautiful that they love, that's bigger than themselves. That's the great thing, but you can't have that unless you're putting it all on the line. You can't experience those great emotions that come with victory unless you're willing to put it all on the line. And when you put it all on the line—all that risk, all that pain—you know what's at stake and you have a great stake in the outcome, and you know that going in."

Then I asked Nate, "When did the quest for a 2019 state championship start?"

"I think it is much more of a continual process than it is an individual season. What spurred all of that? The real answer is that there are a myriad of factors. It was a belief . . . you know when you're trying to believe something but you don't really? We've all been there, where you try to talk yourself into something. In the last three to three and a half years, there was a very deep belief across the board on our football team that we were capable of reaching the goals that we had set—a state championship—and I think that has been the biggest driving force."

Nate put it perfectly, and it was a sentiment I had the privilege of experiencing in my one and only season coaching football at Massillon Washington High School. When you feel like there's no way any team in the state of Ohio has outworked you, then why shouldn't you feel like you have a chance to win a state championship every year? Whether we did or not, that was our goal every year. That's who we were. That's who we'll always be – The Massillon Tigers: 15 for 15.

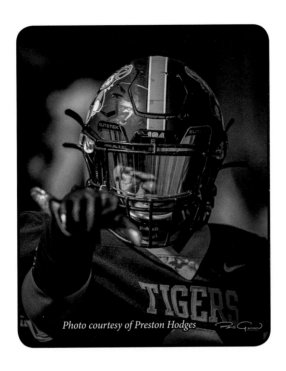

Photo courtesy of Preston Hodges

Photo by Rocky Dorsey

Appendix I
An Open Letter

An open letter from Mr. David Lautenschleger, Washington High School Principal:

My observations as it relates to not only this team, but a lot of successful teams that I have seen and coached are that I always ask many of the kids I have been around, "What's your why?" Answering this question will pretty much lead you typically to the final result of either individual success or team success. If a person's why rests solely in a lot of individual statements regarding their individual success, then it is almost impossible for them to put their focus on a greater goal that would affect a team, a school, and a community.

Individuals who compete with a selfish nature always tend to achieve many personal goals but their singular focus is more on themselves than the team, or the school, or the community they represent. I have noticed truly that when kids on teams start to play for something greater than themselves, such as a teammate, such as their community, or for some other personal motivation greater than themselves, they have answered the question of why?

When your why rests only on your individual statistics and what you want to do for yourself, it is very difficult to selflessly play for a school, or a teammate, or your community, but when something bigger than yourself drives you to compete, you are truly fulfilling life's mission, as to why you are doing what you are doing, and it all relates to the sacrifice for another human being.

This particular senior class, with students like Aidan Longwell, Ethan Tobin—the list goes on and on—they were playing not just for themselves, but for something greater, and that is the most you can ask of anyone who competes. The seniors in this class of 2020 are incredible athletes, but what I got to see every day was their incredible leadership in the hallways, the way they treated people, the way they handled the school respectfully and with a sense of ownership. The truth is much of the success that these kids have achieved in the last couple of years is just the beginning of the success that they are going to have in their futures professionally and personally. They were just laying the groundwork. Their families will thank them later for the sacrifice and the commitment that they've made during these high school years.

As far as Massillon always getting a bad rap, I feel that any time there is a certain level of success achieved on any level there are going to be people who are going to want to take shots at you. But I will tell you that to be successful at anything, you have to be fully committed to the cause. For the people of this community and school district, that cause is the development of successful student athletes who can succeed both in the classroom and on the football field, and can translate their success in one endeavor to success in the other.

It is very difficult for me to comment on any of the negative outside perceptions of the school and program, because I just do not wish to dwell on any of that negativity or that cloud of negative circumstance that people want to create. The truth is, everybody has issues and every school and every district has issues. There is no perfect kid, there is no perfect school, and there is no perfect school district or community. When we start believing that we truly have to begin supporting and respecting the success of all of those communities and athletes around us, true growth will happen in our lives.

After people have found their why in life, it should drive them every minute of every day. Someone's why should drive them to new heights as long as it is front-and-center in their vision and always a prevalent thought.

I really believe in so many of the students whom I have been around at Washington High School. They are resilient, respectful, down-to-earth, and they work hard for what they achieve. That's probably something most people don't realize: that when you combine natural talent with incredible desire to work and outtrain everybody else, eventually there's only a few will be left standing at the top.

Also, I can speak to the alignment piece between my goals as a high school principal and what I want for student-athletes and Coach Moore's goals for what he wants for his student athletes. They are in complete alignment with each other, which enables our arrows to be shot in the same direction with the same speed and the same velocity, so kids understand what the goals and expectations are in his football program and those goals translate into what my expectations are for them in class and in the hallways.

When those two worlds align, it is much easier to find school and program success. It really is an honor to share leadership with great people. I am blessed to share leadership with Coach Moore and so many other great people here at Massillon Washington High School.

Sincerely,
David Lautenschleger
Washington High School Principal

Appendix II
2019 Team Roster

Ben Krichbaum	1	FB/LB	Senior
Robbie Page	2	WR/DB	Senior
Preston Hodges	3	RB/LB	Senior
Jerron Hodges	4	WR/DB	Senior
Aidan Longwell	5	QB	Senior
Terrance Keyes, Jr.	6	RB/DB	Senior
Isaiah Roberson	8	WR/DB	Senior
Jayden Ballard	9	WR/DB	Junior
Anthony Pedro	10	WR/DB	Senior
Seth Lance	11	WR/LB	Senior
Zach Catrone	12	QB	Junior
Eric Thurman	13	WR/LB	Junior
Ahmon Williams	14	WR/DB	Senior
Luke Murphy	15	WR/DB	Senior
Darien Williams	17	WR/DB	Junior
T. J. Williams	19	WR/DB	Junior
Cameron Burgi	20	WR/DB	Junior
Andrew Wilson-Lamp	21	WR/DB	Junior
Daymiere Adams	23	WR/DB	Junior
Nick Liebler	24	FB/LB	Junior
Heath Manson	25	WR/DB	Senior
Raekwon Venson	26	RB/LB	Junior
Zion Phifer	29	RB/FB/LB	Senior
Davon Woods	30	RB/DB	Senior
Isaiah Clark	31	WR/DB	Junior
Xavier Andrews	33	RB/LB	Junior

Andrew Edwards	34	FB/LB	Junior
Jayden Jackson	35	RB/LB	Senior
Peyton Mendenhall	36	FB/LB	Senior
Tyler Friend	40	FB/DL	Senior
Magnus Haines	42	P	Junior
Noah Richards	45	FB/LB	Senior
Davin Wenzel	46	FB/LB	Junior
Dillan Geier	47	FB/DL	Junior
Caiden Woullard	49	FB/LB	Junior
Ethan Tobin	50	OL/DL	Senior
Rager Els	51	OL/DL	Junior
Jacob Orner	53	OL/DL	Junior
Deven Warfield	58	OL/DL	Senior
Devin Hose	59	OL/DL	Senior
Zachary Mundell	60	OL/DL	Junior
Adrian Scott	62	OL/DL	Senior
Nick Grassler	63	OL/DL	Junior
Cole Jones	64	OL/DL	Senior
John Kouth	65	OL/DL	Junior
Niles Cleveland	66	OL/DL	Junior
Terrence Rankl	68	OL/DL	Junior
Dylan Garretson	69	OL/DL	Junior
Alejandro Salazar	72	OL/DL	Senior
Brent Longstreet	73	OL/DL	Junior
Connor Wuske	76	OL/DL	Senior
Manny McElroy	77	OL/DL	Senior
C. J. Harris, Jr.	78	OL/DL	Junior
Jacob Harter	81	WR/DB	Junior
Alex Bauer	89	K	Junior
Kayontea Green	91	WR/DB	Senior
Ryan Schmucker	93	FB/LB	Junior
Corey Campbell	94	FB/DL	Senior
Michael Billman	96	FB/DL	Junior
Levii McLeod	99	FB/LB	Senior

List courtesy of massillontigersathletics.org/

Photo by Rocky Dorsey

Photo by Rocky Dorsey

ACKNOWLEDGMENTS

David Lee Morgan, Jr.'s Thanks

This book would not have been possible without the contributions of the many people who helped inspire me to undertake the project and provided invaluable support all the way through to the end.

As great of an experience as it was to be the varsity running backs coach at Massillon Washington High School, I'm glad my coaching career is over.

With that said, I'd like to thank my wife, *Jill,* for her support and patience during the football season and the months afterward, when all I did was grade papers and work on the book. Thank you, honey. I love you.

Thanks to my parents, *David Lee "Sonny" Morgan, Sr.,* and *Gwen Morgan,* for instilling in me a work ethic that allowed me to accomplish so many things I didn't know I could accomplish.

Thanks to my seven adult kids: *David Lee Morgan, Jr., III* (Trey), *Christian, Brooke, Cameron, Joey, Lunden,* and *Jonah.* You guys are always supportive of my projects. Love you.

Thanks to my sidekick D. J., the greatest chocolate Lab in the world. He kept me company so many nights, just lying at my feet as I typed away. It was fun watching him grow from a pup and celebrating his one-year birthday during all of this.

Thanks to *Scott Ryan* and *David Bushman* and Fayetteville Mafia Press. You guys are amazing, and I can't believe I get to say that I'm represented by such a talented tandem and quality publishing company. Hope there are more projects between us in the future.

Thanks to my dear friend and mentor *Jim Tressel,* who is the president of my alma mater Youngstown State University. I met Coach Tressel in the mideighties when we were both at YSU and he was the head football coach. He later became the head coach at Ohio State. I value our friendship and his wisdom.

Thanks to Coach *Nate Moore* and *Becca Moore* for allowing me the opportunity to coach and write about my experience. You guys are an amazing couple. Thanks for your friendship.

Thanks to the coaching staff—a great bunch of guys who love that school, that team, and that community like their own family.

Thanks to the supporting staff—*Nancy Budner, Olivia Bronczek, Dr. Shaun Doherty, Ron Prunty, Dr. Jared Stefanko, Dr. Tony Perry,* and trainers *Lee Kutz* and *Sam Olewiler.*

Thanks to the Tiger Swing Band staff—*Jason Neel, Jenn Smithhisler, Chris Nussbaum, Jim Unferdorfer, James Gates, Lauren Foster,* and *Bob Wenzel.*

Thanks to cheerleading coach *Kristi Couch* and all the cheerleaders and majorettes.

Thanks to Massillon Mayor *Kathy Catazaro-Perry* and her husband, *Anthony Perry Jr.,* and your family for all you do to make our city an all-American city.

Thanks to equipment manager *Randy Berkley* and his student equipment aides, *Corin Gowin, Chloe Smith, Nathalin Pugh, La Tyvia Henderson,* and *Jayla Woodson,* and student trainer *Bailey Richards.*

Thanks to Superintendent *Paul "Sal" Salvino* and Principal *David Lautenschleger,* who were behind me 100 percent right from the beginning. You guys are amazing men and great leaders in our community.

Thanks to the administration and staff for your support as well.

Thanks to the *David* family for your gracious athletic and academic support throughout the community over the many years.

Thanks to booster club president *Bruce Gallagher* and the entire booster club for support that is second to none.

Thanks to longtime public-address announcer *Walt Bronczek*; to press-box manager *Dave Goff* and his staff, *David Findley, B. J. Burick, Jim Barkan, Sr., Jim Barkan, Jr.,* and *Doug Harmelink*; and to the entire game-day staff at Paul Brown Tiger Stadium—all of whom make home games feel like a major Division I college football experience.

Thanks to *Rocky Dorsey* and *Bill Garman* for providing the photos that bring the stories to life.

Thanks to my English department colleagues for your help in the classroom.

Thanks to my "TBT" squad—*Adam Calhoun, Spencer Leno, Alyssa Meissner, Carla Mangle* and *Julie Reinhart*—for our lively and colorful Wednesday-morning meetings.

Thanks to Assistant Principal *Renee Parr,* who is always sporting a friendly, warm smile. Being a former English teacher, she loved just sitting in on our classes to get her English fix.

Thanks to the members of the Massillon Board of Education for providing our students with a quality educational experience. And to *Beau Rugg* from the OHSAA.

Thanks to the *Longwell* Family for the great hospitality.

Thanks to MCTV for your outstanding coverage.

Thanks to Assistant Athletic Director *Brian "Bubba" Pachis,* and ticket-office managers *Michelle Wolfe* and *Pat Mozingo.*

And thanks to *Jamey Palma, Tony Thornsberry, Dave Scheetz, Matt Ferrell,* and the entire media production department at WHS and Accent, which does an amazing job broadcasting not only our football games, but basketball as well.

Thanks to Mike and Kim Gifford for their help and support.

There are so many more people I'd like to thank, but I'm afraid I will miss so many of you, so just know that if you know me, I thank you for your support and friendship. Go Tigers!

ACKNOWLEDGMENTS

Scott Ryan's Thanks

I have to thank the *Black Swarm Podcast* for interviewing David Lee Morgan, Jr. I wanted to do a book about the Massillon Tigers for years, but I am such a lifelong fan, I knew I couldn't be objective. When I heard David on the podcast, I knew I finally found the author I had been looking for. I have been sitting in Section 14, Row S, Seats 1-4 my entire life. My dad (see first picture, taken in 1997) and I went to the games with my mother and brother back in the day. Now I go with my wife and son. (See picture taken at the 2019 state game.) I am a Tiger through and through and the team means the world to me. We didn't set out to tell the entire story, because that book can't be told. Everyone has their own version of the 2019 season, and *all the other* seasons. In Massillon, we live for our Tigers (even when we move away to Columbus). David did a great job of taking us through this season through his eyes. I am thankful for so many people whom I will list in a moment, but I dedicate my work on the book to my dad and my son. I sat with both of them at games and that is what being a Tiger is about to me: *family*. Mike Ryan. Scott Ryan. Alex Ryan.

Thanks to *David Lee Morgan, Jr.,* for all the calls and all the fun. Thanks for sharing your vision and opening your world to the world. In return, I gave him his first bite of Kraus' Pizza, and I think he still owes me.

Thanks to *Kraus' Pizza,* because why not.

Thanks to *Becca Moore* for all the support. I asked her for one sentence about Massillon/McKinley Week; she gave me four pages. She is the first lady of Massillon and the kindest person I know. Go exercise.

Thanks to *Nate Moore* and all the coaches for the extra quotes and photos and for giving me a fun 2018-2019 football season.

If *Ellery Moore* ever asks you to call him, call him. You won't be disappointed.

Ray Wise, you made it in the book, now stop telling me you beat Massillon.

Thanks to every *player, parent,* and *Tiger supporter* of 2019.

Thanks to *Chris Easterling* and *The Independent* for all the hard work covering the Tigers and for sharing your words.

Thanks to *Erik Longwell* for raising Aidan and for all the photos in the book. We had a fun call talking Tiger history.

Thanks to *Rocky Dorsey* for bringing the book alive with his photos and openly sharing his art.

Thanks to *Wayne Barnes* for a great cover and the push-up art.

Thanks to *Dan Studer* and everyone who supplied photos for the book.

Thanks to *Howard's Tiger Rags* and *Simon Says Promotions* for helping support the book.

Thanks to *David Bushman* for the edits and for being a great copublisher.

Thanks to *Alex Ryan* for all the edits and for going to the games with me.

Thanks to *Todd "Huppie" Huppert* for being a first reader.

Thanks to *Gillian Surber* for sorting photos and being my favorite Surber.

Thanks to *Joyce Ryan* for being the best mom and always helping me out.

Thanks to my friends: *Lisa Hession, Erin O'Neil, Janet Jarnagin, Courtenay Stallings, Lisa Mercado-Fernandez, Holly Brothers, Mindy Fortune, Tony Stanic,* and *Joshua Minton.* I couldn't create art without each of you.

Thanks to my wife, *Jen Ryan,* who when we met said, "We have to drive two hours to watch a high school football game every week?" And now she yells, "T-I-G!" as if she graduated from Massillon. I love you.

> *"Be kind to me or treat me mean. I'll make the most of it,*
> *I'm an extraordinary machine."* — Fiona Apple

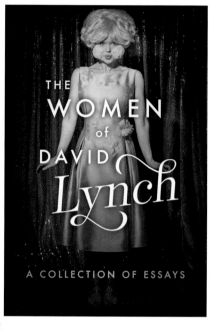
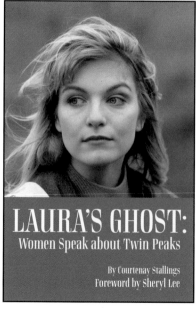

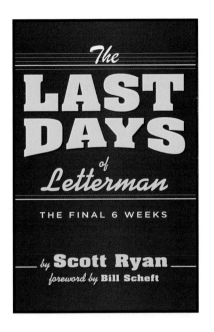

Read an inside look at the final six weeks of *Late Show with David Letterman,* all told through the words of the staff that wrote, directed, and produced those iconic last twenty-eight episodes in 2015. *The Last Days of Letterman* by Scott Ryan

ISBN: 9781949024005

Mark Frost cocreated *Twin Peaks*, wrote for *Hill Street Blues,* and has written over ten novels. Learn about his life, his craft, and his career in this new book by David Bushman.

ISBN: 9781949024104

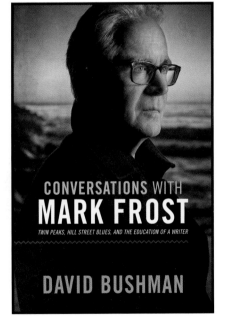

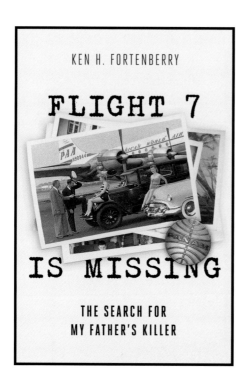

Ken Fortenberry solves one of the greatest real-life mysteries in aviation history as he searches for the killer of his father and the cause of the crash of Flight 7.

ISBN: 9781949024067

Scarlett Harris takes a deep dive into the world of female wrestling and some of the greatest characters in all of sports. This book will be released in February 2021.

ISBN: 9781949024180